Back
to
Abnormal

Books by Caskie Stinnett

WILL NOT RUN FEBRUARY 22ND

OUT OF THE RED

Back

to

Abnormal

By Caskie Stinnett

PUBLISHED BY

BERNARD GEIS ASSOCIATES

DISTRIBUTED BY RANDOM HOUSE

Library of Congress Catalog Card Number: 63-18455

Manufactured in the United States of America

First Printing

All of the articles, essays, and comment in this book appeared originally in *Speaking of Holiday,* an unorthodox and highly personal publication which dealt with the writers, editors, and illustrators of *Holiday.*

To Loni
Who Shared This Period

Contents

A Note to the Reader

The essays that follow represent a sort of criticism that is wide-ranging and urgent and confessedly polemical. They were written in a variety of moods. Some are angry, some jubilant, some exhortative, some despairing. There is one thing that you must remember when reading essays and that is, when a man sits down to compose an essay he becomes an evangelist; he detects wrong-doing—or wrong-thinking, anyway—and he seeks to lead you into paths of righteousness. What he neglects to say, though, is that his views are narrowly personal, nor does he even suggest that he may be no closer to the truth than the next man. That would defeat the purpose of the essay. The feeling he really wishes to impart is that you are not reading the imprint of type upon paper, but rather words that have been chiseled into stone. It's a struggle to resist calling the first chapter Genesis.

With few exceptions, the pieces that follow do not represent my preferences for subjects, or perhaps it would be simpler to say that these were not the things that I wanted most to write about at the time. My notion of a fine subject to write about is a brook meandering through a meadow in the springtime; the water is clear and cold, the grass is green, and there is the odor of wild onions in the air. (If I had the time, I'd finish that piece right now.) Or how it feels to stand under the overhang of a barn, waiting for a sudden summer storm to end so you can get back to the job that was interrupted by those first big drops that fell so heavily around you. Or to walk a hedgerow with a dog in the first snowfall of the season, hoping it will turn into a real blizzard but knowing in your heart that it will probably end before you get back to the house.

All of these subjects I have just mentioned deal with the country. It's my abiding conviction that people who live in cities are crazy; if they aren't crazy to begin with, they ultimately grow crazy. I live in the biggest city in the world.

These pieces, as essays almost invariably do, evolved from situations. I doubt if anyone ever said, "I think I'll sit down after dinner tonight and write an essay about something." No, it doesn't happen that way. Rather, you've seen something that stirred you, or you feel grief or humiliation or outrage or triumph, and the first thing you know you're writing about it. The essayist is permitted practically no selectivity of subject matter; he's incident-prone.

Finally, I'd like to say that this book makes no claim to being the last word on these subjects, nor is it any closer to being the first one. Man's capacity for indignation, as well as his provocation, seems likely to increase in the years ahead and these subjects will all be worked over again, and more effectively. There will always be essayists and they will always be repeating to themselves the words spoken by Napoleon after the surrender of Paris: "Wherever I am not, nothing but folly is committed." He derives from this a bracing sense of intellectual and moral rigor. Be as patient with him as you can.

CASKIE STINNETT

New York City

Back
to
Abnormal

1

A Feast of Nonsense

TELL US YOUR PROBLEM, BUT KEEP WALKING

This is a great country, where everyone has the right to vote for the Kennedy of his choice, and we'd like to keep it this way. But a headline in the Los Angeles *Times* has recently introduced a gnawing note of anxiety to our life. "New Walk-in Mental Health Center Opens Here," the *Times* announces.

We are all for mental health, don't get us wrong. Physically, we're go, but we sometimes wake up with a coated tongue *mentally,* so we try to keep in touch with new developments in the field, just as an ulcer case or an arthritic scans the leading medical journals such as *Reader's Digest* for some radical new treatment. Well, the walk-in concept—where the patient emerges, we presume, whistling—is radical, but has it been carefully thought out? What we're really trying to get at is whether we're ready to let the couch go as a symbol of security.

[3

We'd like to kick this thing around a little. In the first place, Los Angeles is a yeasty and restless city, and inclined to be a little impulsive. Things happen fast there, and we guess it's only natural that when a fellow has a little problem going that makes him want to slash his wrists, he'd either like to get on with it or get over it, but in a hurry in either case. For him, the Walk-in or Instant Mental Health Center seems ideal. If lucky, perhaps, he could wrap the whole thing up during his lunch hour. Or, we can even imagine a movie starlet, with a few nagging emotional problems, telling her date to pick her up an hour later for dinner. "I'll think you'll be surprised," she says mysteriously. It sounds good, but it has some of the qualities of a script turned out by one of the Culver City or Burbank studios.

If we know Los Angeles, the center isn't going to long remain a Walk-in service. It's going to be a Drive-in, and the patient will get a mental toning-up without turning off his ignition. It's not beyond possibility that a car-wash be operated in conjunction with the enterprise, but we must admit that here we're just thinking out loud. (It just goes to show how your mind starts working once you get onto the Los Angeles scheme of things.)

The center will limit its service to six visits for each individual and will be known—would we make it up?—as the Rush Center. It was named for Benjamin Rush, but some remarkable coincidences occur in Los Angeles, and this is undoubtedly one of them. Whether six visits would be enough to prepare a man for his bumpy journey down the highway of life is something we aren't qualified to judge, but there is an impatient, masochistic quality to the city and its people, and we imagine the pace was set by the unconscious rhythm of life there.

James Thurber, a man with an uncommonly clear head, was once speaking to us of the American admiration for size. For reasons which he said were murky to him, the people of this country insist upon having the largest cars, the tallest buildings, the biggest city, and we even want our women to possess the most spectacular measurements. Well, California is fast becoming our most populous state, and it has always done things in a big way. If it has also managed to create the grandest neurosis, we hope the Rush Center keeps pace and becomes the sort of Walk-in Mental Health Center that Cecil B. De Mille would have built. There should certainly be a measure of consolation, too, in belonging to an aristocracy of neurotics.

WE'LL JUST KEEP OUR COAT, IF YOU DON'T MIND

We read just about everything but we have an especial fondness for the ladies' magazines whose contributions to *la dolce vita* we find endlessly fascinating. For example: "Make an orange cup by turning an orange peel inside out. After-dinner coffee aflame in orange cups will make your dinner unforgettable. Saturate a cube of sugar in a spoon with brandy, light, and float in coffee. Then stand back for the 'ooh's' and 'aah's' when you enter the darkened room with the flaming orange cups."

Well, the first thing you will notice about a man who has recently had coffee aflame in an orange cup is that he's changed somehow. He seems older, his hair and eyebrows are shorter, his hands tremble slightly, and there's an uneasy look in his eyes. Chances are that he's also wearing a brand-new suit of clothes.

We've never lifted an orange peel full of coffee, but we've used the paper cups they have on trains and they aren't even safe with water in them. We would pick up an orange peel full of flaming coffee only with tongs, and if available, we'd like an asbestos glove. The author of this orange-peel suggestion chose her words with uncanny accuracy. We don't know anything that will make a meal more "unforgettable" than some flaming coffee in the lap.

It's our guess that the really smart guests will get their coats and go home as soon as the lights go out. That's the tip-off that something unusual is in the works and that it will likely involve fire. But if you're still sitting there when the inferno is brought in on a tray, we can only say that we have a grudging admiration for your courage and your determination to taste orange coffee. Also life fully.

We think the author is wrong, though, about the "ooh's" and "aah's" she expects to hear from her guests. Once a few of those orange peels collapse, you aren't going to hear "ooh's" and "aah's," lady. You're going to hear words that wouldn't be tolerated in the forecastle of a freighter.

HOW TO KICK THE READING HABIT

It can only be classified as foolhardy for a person engaged in the flimsy business of writing books, as we are, to direct hostile words at book critics, but that's exactly what we propose to do. (In Max Beerbohm's "Letter From a Young Man Refusing to Pay His Tailor's Bill," he writes: "Mr. Eustace Davenport has received the half-servile, half-insolent screed which Mr. Yardley has addressed to him. Let Mr. Yardley cease from crawling on his knees and shaking his fist. . . ." The message is not lost upon us, but we have no book pending at the moment.)

Actually, this is a review of a book review written by Elizabeth Janeway in *The New York Times Book Review*. The criticism deal with a thoroughly delightful novel (there you have *our* estimate of it) by Elizabeth Spencer titled *The Light in the Piazza* (McGraw-Hill). Miss Janeway addresses a book much the same way that a bulldozer attacks a strip mine, and to show you what she has done to the book, it will be necessary to tell you a little bit about the book itself. An American lady has taken her grown daughter, an exquisite girl who, because of an accident, has been left with the mind of a ten-year-old, to Florence, where a romance promptly develops between the daughter and a handsome young Italian. The dilemma of the mother is hardly obscure, and it is on the thorny question of should or should not she permit the marriage that the story is built.

Having some consideration for the readers of this charming book, as well as for the author, we would never dream of telling you whether or not the marriage took place, but it is with a heavy heart that we must report that Miss Janeway was troubled by no such misgivings. Midway through her review, Miss Janeway blithely announces: "Clara is blissfully married, and her new family carry her off to the safety of the seraglio." Anybody around here still interested in reading the book?

Curious as to how Miss Janeway confused a synopsis with a review, we read with great interest a short essay on book reviewing by Francis Brown, editor of the *Times Book Review,* in the Authors Guild *Bulletin.* In fairness to everyone, we must admit that Mr. Brown discussed the art of literary criticism in a scholarly and interesting manner, and we found nothing that would indicate Miss Janeway was following his instructions in synopsizing *The Light in the Piazza.* Nothing, that is, except for one sentence in the next to last paragraph of the piece, when Mr. Brown says the reviewer "shares his discoveries with his reader." Just to please us—as well as all other novelists we know—we wonder if Mr. Brown would amend that to say that the reviewer "shares *some* of his discoveries with his reader."

To suggest that Miss Spencer's betrayal was no isolated case and that the *Times Book Review* is not the only offender, we would like to report the experience of Richard Bissell, author of *A Stretch on the River, 7½ Cents, Say, Darling* and, more recently, *Good Bye, Ava* (Little, Brown). A few months ago in these pages we described *Good Bye, Ava* as first-rate reading but expressed the fear that, as so often happens, the book critics would review not this book but an earlier one. In reply to this, Mr. Bissell has deposed as follows:

"Yes, I got a liberal number of reviews of books I wrote ten years ago instead of the one under scrutiny. Also a large number of reviews consisting of complete synopses of the plot including denouement and finale. Jesus!"

SIC TRANSIT GLORIA

We doubt if there is anyone around who doesn't know that the Government has three layers of classified documents,

Confidential, Secret, and Top Secret, and that certain agencies are assigned the privilege of using certain classifications.
Well, he who giveth can also taketh away, and it is with a
heavy heart that we must tell you that last week the Government stripped an agency of the right to use Top Secret. The
agency was the Civil War Centennial Commission.

MUSIC NOTE

We once relayed the report of our record-shop observer that a recording was being featured with the title, "Bon
Voyage, Titanic." He's just checked in again, this time with
the news of a new album. It's called, "Sing Along with
Charles DeGaulle."

WHAT SILENCE AT APPOMATTOX?

A few years ago we read some Civil War books, hoping
they would act as a sort of mithridate, but as the publishers'
lists became clogged with novels, biographies, chronicles,
anthologies, and volumes of letters—all concerned with the
period of 1861–1865—we said the hell with it and gave up.
No war could be that fascinating.

Besides, there were other things to turn to. You could take
your choice of several books about the Reverend Peter
Marshall, the power of positive thinking was undiminished,
and if you possessed a curiosity about sin, New England style,
there was always *Peyton Place*. Now absolute darkness has
just about set in; it's either read about the Civil War or else
sit up and listen to records. Right now we're reading a book
called *How to Detect Enemy Planes*. It isn't good, but it isn't
the Civil War, either.

Just before writing this, we glanced at an up-to-date bibli-
ography of Civil War works, and we were struck by the
thought that there are only five or six books still to be
written on this subject. (Maybe we're already too late; Civil

War writers, we've noticed, strike with the speed of a hungry cobra.) These gaps in an otherwise complete chronicle follow:

Suggested Title	Description of Book
Unpublished Letter of Stonewall Jackson	The *only* remaining unpublished letter of this famous general, written to an aunt when he was fifteen, expressing gratitude for an unidentified Christmas present. Complete with maps of the Valley Campaign.
Moment of Decision	A factual account of the period in Gen. J. E. B. Stuart's life, extending from 3:00 P.M. to 3:40 P.M., August 8, 1861. During this period, Stuart inspected a field kitchen. Illus.
Silent Night	An anthology of Civil War *Christmas* stories. There have been anthologies of Christmas stories, but this volume contains over 3,000 Civil War Christmas stories. End paper illustration of Santa Claus exchanging hats with Gen. R. E. Lee.
Eagle of the Confederacy	What would have happened if Gen. John B. Gordon, dashing young Confederate, had possessed an air force? This book speculates on the course of the war under those circumstances. Illustrated with drawings of aerial bombardment of Fort Sumter.
Lee, as My Father Knew Him	Written by the son of one of Gen. R. E. Lee's orderlies, this book is an analysis of the contents of Lee's pockets on the day he rode into Appomattox to surrender to Gen. Grant.

CIVIL?

A few days ago we read some more about that centennial—thirty-three states now have Civil War Commissions energetically engaged in putting together shows, pageants, spectacles, and battle re-enactments to celebrate the Civil War Centennial. If there are many people who feel about the Civil War as we do, this could easily bring on another one.

The center of this furious activity, oddly enough, is in the South. When we asked a Southern friend of ours for an explanation of this, he replied rather feverishly: "Son, this is *our* war." Perhaps we've overlooked some very significant fact in a tangled situation, but for the South to glorify the Civil War seems to us to be roughly equivalent to Max Schmeling erecting a monument at Yankee Stadium on the spot where Joe Louis beat the hell out of him. While Schmeling slumbered peacefully amid murmurs of "Don't he look natural?" there seems little doubt that he was inhabiting an Appomattox of his own.

We have watched apprehensively as biographies of Forrest and Pickett began to nudge Art Linkletter and other great contemporary writers from choice positions in the bookstores, and there was no diminishing of our anxiety when we first noticed some familiar sheriffs and cattle rustlers of television serials reappearing on other channels as Federal cavalrymen. No sooner had these actors brought peace to a gun-weary cattle town or recovered the ranch from the crooked banker than they showed up in the glare of Fort Sumter or running a message from General Lee to General Beauregard. Somewhere along the two-thousand-mile-eastward trip, they passed Wardrobe.

Not long ago, the Civil War Round Table of Washington, D.C., held a dinner meeting, the menu for which consisted of pokeberries and green apples marinated in stump juice, young horse-corn leaves, sassafras root and bacon fat, stolen turkey and chitterlings, ground acorns and swamp cress, hardtack and corn pone, and, for dessert, souffled wild onions. Things are going to get worse before they get better.

Previously we called attention to the flood of Civil War books which has rolled from the presses during the past few years and listed the titles which we felt remained to be published. Circumstances have led us to re-examine this list, and we feel that we can make a few additions to plug up a hole previously overlooked. The attrition of subjects has taken its toll, and authors are now being forced to associate their subjects with current events in a way that we did not anticipate. Books still to be written include:

Polk Medicine. Home remedies suggested to his troops by General Leonidas Polk.

Dear and Glorious Position. Grant's army holds Richmond in siege.

The War Lovers. The master plan for the Civil War Centennial celebration.

Edwin Stanton—the Admiral Strauss of the Civil War.

The Presidency: from Abraham Lincoln to James C. Hagerty. A study in executive responsibility. Illustrated.

In conclusion, we would like to quote Mort Sahl, a man with a clear eye and a cool head. In noting that ABC has announced plans to do twelve shows on the Civil War, Sahl said: "With the current leadership in Washington, if they wait six months, they can do them *live.*"

OFFBEAT

It has always been a high mystery to us how a school of literature gets started, and we are more perplexed than usual over the limited success of what has come to be known as the San Francisco or beatnik group. We say "limited" because it is quite likely that Mr. Kingsley Amis, the English author, may have damaged the standing of the spokesman of this literary disarray—Mr. Jack Kerouac, whose first few novels advanced him high on the list of noteworthy contemporary writers. In a recent essay, which was surgical from start to finish, Amis described how, before appearing on a panel with Kerouac, he had been instructed "that Mr. Kerouac was very nice provided he was convinced that those present were on his side, felt sympathetic to him, in short liked him." He then related how Mr. Kerouac insulted both him and Ashley Montagu, another panelist, "without giving us the chance to tell him how much we liked him."

Although Kerouac may have a poor grasp of the rules of social conduct, he has undoubtedly written some arresting stuff, and we go along with the contention that a writer should be judged by his writing rather than his behavior. The beatnik movement itself is something else again, and a puzzle at that, and we can only assume that writers and audience got together in the way that everything is created to fill a need. As lemon was created for Dover sole, for example.

Kenneth Rexroth, who rose from the cellar-nightclubs of San Francisco to become poet laureate of the beatniks, is difficult for us to classify because we try to keep things straight, and to be thoroughly honest we seldom know what the hell he is talking about. In leafing through *The Art of Worldy Wisdom,* a book of Mr. Rexroth's poetry, we came across a poem called "Fundamental Disagreement with Two Contemporaries." It's simply terrible.

Perhaps the third most important member of the San Francisco group (it may be that we have our order all wrong; if so we pray forgiveness) is Allen Ginsberg, author of *Howl, and Other Poems.* From the title this seems to be the kind of book that once you put it down, you can't pick it up again.

We doubt that this is San Francisco's finest hour.

ALL I CAN SAY IS . . . (SOB)
THANK YOU

The entertainment industry has honored its own through the bestowal of Oscars, Emmies, Tonies, and Obies (*Obie* for Off-Broadway, get it?), to say nothing of Drama Critics Circle, Peabody, and various other awards, and if there is anyone around who didn't win something, please hold up your hand. On an enterprise of such monumental scale, accidents are bound to happen.

We've watched this parade to the podium of actors, electricians, directors, and unidentified men in evening dress smoking cigars, and we must admit that ours was a jaundiced eye, indeed. The participants always seem to be taking it seriously, that much is obvious, but the whole proceedings have

the flavor of one of those show business gags that is always
good for a laugh in the trade but which falls flat in the laps
of the studio audience. In our line of business (writing),
there are three notable awards each year—the Pulitzer Prize,
the Nobel Prize, and the National Book Award—and these
are awarded to authors after thorough study has been made
of their talent, their purpose, and their contribution to contemporary literature. The awards are meaningful, and this so
dominates our approach to industry awards that perhaps we
should disqualify ourselves from judging those outside of our
own field. When John Cheever or Wright Morris or Bruce
Catton get the National Book Award, we know it is not because they are nice fellows (they may be, at that) or are well
known around Sardi's or Chasen's, but rather that their work
has withstood the close scrutiny of critics and scholars and the
work—not the writer—is thought to be the best.

The fascinating if somewhat bewildering aspect of the
Oscar and Emmy awards ceremonies is the casual attitude
demonstrated by the motion picture and television people
toward the categories which they have established. The Academy of Television Arts and Sciences, at whose convocation
the Emmies are awarded, honored Fred Astaire for what
they declared to be "the best dramatic performance" of the
year. Paul Muni and Rod Steiger, both nominated in the
same category, lost out, presumably on the ground that where
real acting was concerned they just weren't in Astaire's league.
Not bad, you understand, just outclassed. A few days later,
after going over his collection of Emmies and noticing the
strange one, Astaire fished it out and sent it back to the
Faculty. That ended the matter until next year when, presumably, it will be awarded to Miss Dinah Shore, the famous
actress.

So far as viewer attractions (a trade term, not ours) are
concerned, the Oscar and Emmy ceremonies are outranked
for us only by the first two or three days of a national political
convention (the period, preceding the nominations, when
local mayors welcome the delegates and local fife and bugle
corps execute their snappy formations) or the first couple of

days of the Miss America beauty pageant. The suspense of these events, at this stage, is unbearable for a sensitive man. Perhaps we should also place in this class books with such titles as *Crocodiles and Other People* and *Eighteenth Century German Porcelain.*

We don't know how many categories were finally recognized at the Emmy ceremony because our eyes glazed over and we lost the struggle to keep awake, but we duly noted a few days later that a spokesman for the Academy had come out for reform by suggesting the whole thing be reduced to only twelve classifications. This is the sort of suggestion that is guaranteed to drive the planners of these events crazy but it exactly suits our temperament. The only other thing to cause us anxiety is that we were just informed that Harper's is bringing out a book called *Steps in Time,* the autobiography of Fred Astaire. You don't suppose . . . no, it couldn't happen.

MEANWHILE, BACK IN POTTSTOWN

We've been rather silent on the subject of the long novel, holding our comment until other precincts had reported in and hoping (we've never entirely lost the innocent optimism of our youth) that something would happen to discourage authors from describing in the most wearisome detail the designs in the carpets of the characters' boyhood homes. But no. Novels are getting longer, and the designs in the carpets are more complex. Writers have confused weight of manuscript with weight of message; if a book is longer than *War and Peace,* it's better than *War and Peace.*

In 1900 and thereabouts, novels ran to 324 pages and any publisher who went much beyond that was throwing caution to the wind. A buyer browsing in a book store could pick up a volume, take a quick glance at the frontispiece to see if the action suited his taste, and depart, comfortable in the knowledge that he had acquired an evening's entertainment rather than a test of his endurance. Now we have books so large it would be more appropriate to fix their price by the pound, in much the same way that bacon is bought. The value of books seems to be based on the physical material involved; 900 pages of anything costs more than 500 pages of anything. There's nothing abstract about that concept.

Try as we might, though, we cannot shake the old-fashioned conviction that form is important in the novel. J. D. Salinger required only 277 tightly written pages for *Catcher in the Rye* (Little, Brown and Company), one of the most haunting novels we have ever read, and Mark Harris, an economical writer if there ever was one, brought in *There's Something about a Soldier* (Macmillan) in 175 pages, or, to be exact, 174½. In both cases, of course, the authors sacrificed some details that John O'Hara, for example, found essential to the movement of *From the Terrace* (Random House). Among these were such arresting bits of information as: Jean Rothermel's brother, Tom, skipped a grade in school in 1908; Tom's father had a gold watch and chain and gold cuff buttons; and the invocation at Alfred's commencement was pronounced by an assistant rector, rather than the rector. In describing Benziger's office, O'Hara calls attention to the fact that "the paperweights were lumps of sculped polished anthracite and a varnished spragger, and there were calendars and foot rules bearing the names of firms that supplied the Mountain City Coal Company with dynamite, cable, dualin caps, electric locomotives and such." There are 897 pages of that, which figures out (for those not owning a pencil) to only three pages less than 900.

A few days ago we found ourselves speaking contentiously on this subject to two of the big-book novelists, and we were disconcerted to find that they felt they had nothing to defend. "This is the true novel form," one of them said blandly, and for a crowded second we had the feeling of witnessing an epiphany.

It has just occurred to us that a best-selling novel is now within reach of all writers. The components are well known and not too much skill should be required in the mixing. Against a wartime background (preferably the Civil War; why take chances?) weave the life story of a handsome middle-aged woman who has an uncontrollable desire for eleven-year-old boys, add a mistreated Negro, a communist (this may require a bit of doing if the period embraces the Civil War, but you'll have to work some of these things out for yourself), and a thinly disguised F. Scott Fitzgerald. Then provide about 850 pages of lavish detail, taking pains to establish the fact that the handsome middle-aged lady skipped a grade in school, and when Scott said good-by to Princeton not even the *assistant* rector showed up. The title that occurs to us is *The Ugly American Pushes Lolita from the Terrace.* But we're only thinking out loud, mind you.

WE TAKE GREAT PLEASURE IN PRESENTING . . .

America to us is a land of hope, opportunity, and an annual award for everybody. There's a shrill minority now claiming that we've overdone the award business and they point for justification to the awards given each year in the fields of journalism, literature, the theater, and motion pictures. We want it clearly understood that we have nothing to do with this line of thinking; indeed, we don't think we've gone far enough. We've been watching the awards pretty carefully for the last few months—we have our meals sent in on a tray—and we find several fields completely overlooked. In order to tighten this thing up, we're offering the following awards which are open to everybody except our relatives, of course, and the boy who comes in once a month to do our writing for us.

1. The Halohydrocarbonoclasticus Award for outstanding achievement in the field of sulfate-reducing desulfovibrios.

AWARD: No cash award, but a neat gilt statuette, comma-shaped like the bacteria, goes each year to the winner.

2. The Outstanding Achievement Award for people who have failed to qualify for any other award. The winner must claim achievement (*outstanding* achievement, that is) in any one of the following fields:

1. Weather guessing
2. Two-finger whistling

3. Uninterrupted sleep

4. Length of time watching free television show on one glass of beer.

AWARD: Our own personal check for ten dollars, or one dollar in cash.

3. The Sick-Half-The-Time Award for outstanding achievement in the field of hypochondria. (To preserve some semblance of order in this award, competition must be restricted to *employed* men and women. Idle or retired persons hold such an obvious advantage over other contestants that they must be disqualified as full-time or professional hypo- chondriacs.)

AWARD: One free basal metabolism.

There, that covers everything.

FOOD'S PARADISE

Just about the only comforting aspect to the sudden evolution of self-styled gourmets in the country is the fact that many of them eat themselves into a reasonably sound sleep early in the evening, and aside from an occasional belch or two, the rest of the party is spared the boredom of their presence. We hail this human frailty, this inability to gorge and still discourse, because of the hours of agony it has saved us—the recollections of *truite au bleu* in the little cafe in Lyons, the indescribable eggplant *imambaildi* in the taverna in Athens, and the unsurpassed *cannelloni* in the restaurant at Naples. That it's foolish to try to outwit our arteries is incontrovertible; the human relationship is even less durable. This obiter dictum, we would point out here, is not addressed to the person of cultivated taste who quietly enjoys good food but rather to the snob who is taking a short cut to culture and who doesn't know a sauce from the caulking of a boat.

It may be that our tolerance for this sort of thing has suddenly declined, but it seems to us that the fellow who a few years ago was smacking his lips over peanut butter is now out in the kitchen telling the chef how to make a really transcendent bearnaise. And the worst of it is that he doesn't stop with the chef; he wants to tell the other guests too. A friend of ours—a friend, now, once removed—has a viscera that would easily accommodate tinfoil, yet we were not surprised when lunching with him a few weeks ago to see him approach a scaloppine in an almost Priapic way. After delivering a highly misleading lecture on the proper way to prepare a veal, he consumed it with a speed that would have made Brillat-Savarin quit the kitchen forever. Then came the mopping-up operation—a final obscenity—that consisted of blotting up the residue of scaloppine sauce with chunks of bread which were conveyed to his mouth with the regularity, and almost the same sound effects, of coal moving on a bucket belt. As he paid his check and selected a toothpick, he introduced himself to the manager—an integral part of the gourmet ritual, we've learned—and confessed that life had presented him with only two scaloppines he could classify as better. Since we had to get back to the office, we decided to take a total loss on the story but our ears picked up the word "Naples" as we went through the door.

And if, like Pavlov's dogs, they begin to salivate at the sound of a bell, the new food experts respond even more readily to the sound of a cork leaving a bottle. Wine, as anyone knows who has progressed beyond Schrafft's, is a symbol of status, and anyone who turns his glass down is either a savage or is eating breakfast. We've seen groups assembled around such gastronomical triumphs as creamed tuna fish or fried haddock, arguing the merits of a sauterne as opposed to a chablis. Even after *that* is settled, a lively argument is likely to break out over whether the bottle should be chilled, served at room temperature, or even heated to body warmth of 98.6 degrees. For one in the group to order milk or iced tea, for example, would be roughly equivalent to suggesting to a group at Birdland that they all go over to the Roosevelt Grill to hear a few sets by Guy Lombardo.

The origin of the gourmet compulsion is obscured by the swirling mists of fashion, and we have no idea why a man should feel that the deification of his stomach will bring him social salvation. All we're sure of is that an encounter with one more gourmet who prefers offal—whether sweetbreads, tripe, or brains—to a well-broiled steak or lobster is all that we need to drive us back to Howard Johnson's.

OH MEN! OH WOMEN!

We have a deep-seated admiration and respect for women. You don't have to read between the lines, or search out hidden meanings, to be struck by that fact. But knowing the wisdom of women, we've been a little disturbed by the strange dichotomy in their personality that permits them to be lulled into contentment by the baby talk which they encounter in their fashion publications.

For example, would we ever start to town wearing a little number of lively plaid cotton with a sweetly curving neckline that fastens in a flattering bow-and-lacing arrangement and a snug, set-in waistband and dirndl skirt? Frankly, no. We wouldn't be caught dead in it. And would we go to the beach wearing a breeze-cool bare-backed cotton aralac of multicolored checks made with a flirty ruffle and whopping big pockets crisply trimmed with white, wide rickrack? We would only if we intended to keep walking into the ocean until our pert little open-back half-bonnet of oh-so-soft black velvet started floating.

Another thing we would keep away from is a hostess coat which gives us both glamor and warmth and brings pure enchantment. Rather than go through the hostess-coat period of the day, we think we would prefer going straight to bed, making a special point of not giving our face any kind of cocktail, followed by a lather facial of our favorite complexion soap. We're positive that if we worked the lather in thoroughly, rinsed with warm water, splashed with cold, and patted gently with a slice of cucumber, it would not leave our face wondering why we had not tried this creamy lather, so soft and smooth, before. It would leave our face wondering why we didn't try Alcoholics Anonymous.

Before going to bed we would take care *not* to kick off our oomphies, toasties, softies, flatties, or any other lounging slippers with foam-cushiony sole that are made for eye-appeal and cozy comfort. We would sit on the edge of the bed and drop our shoes as we always do, and if the people downstairs want to pound on the radiator in protest that's all right too.

There are a few things we would be certain to do, though, and this is a good time to get these in the record. We would fight off sleep long enough to get all of the Raven's Blood nail lacquer off our hands, if we had to soak them in Scotch whisky to do it. Then we would stick our head under the shower to wash off the egg-and-vinegar hair-conditioning, and it should be only a minute before we were rid of the season's most exciting new lipstick—Guillotine Red.

Then we could go to bed and sleep.

IT ISN'T THE HEAT, IT'S THE STUPIDITY

There's nothing monotheistic about us. Our destiny is controlled by many gods, and right now Helios is putting us up to some mischief that we know will lead us away from salvation and not toward it. Irritability, we have discovered, mounts with the thermometer; petty annoyances of the spring and winter, when examined in ninety-degree weather, suddenly appear intolerable. Injustice cries out for correction, not even waiting for the station break. A few days ago, during the worst of June's first fierce heat wave, we opened a drawer into which we had stuffed an accumulation of clippings and began to finger the contents. Each clipping bespoke a transgression, and we plan to expose the transgressors, here and now, before the promised cold front arrives.

The first clipping (i.e. the first in the enormity of its offense) was headed "Film to Get Premiere in N.Y. Prison," and related how a movie, called *Public Pigeon No. 1* was due to have its world premiere in Greenhaven Prison at Stormville, N.Y., where all prisoners would be required to see it. Well, we hold to the old-fashioned notion that prisoners are practically human, and we also have trouble erasing from our mind that fragment of the Eighth Amendment forbidding the infliction of cruel and unusual punishment. The last paragraph of the clipping explained that Greenhaven is a maximum security prison, the walls of which are embedded from thirty to forty feet below ground to prevent tunneling. This struck us as a highly relevant addition to the story.

It's no jump at all to the next clipping, which tells, with a poorly contrived aura of mystery, that the Academy Award for the best screenplay of 1956 went to *The Brave One,* a film whose author could not be found, and indeed, could not even be properly identified. Subsequent news stories hinted darkly that the writer was really one of Hollywood's Unfriendly Ten, writing under a fictitious name and for that reason couldn't come forward. The matter stood at this state of balance for us, rumor struggling against uninformative announcements, until we chanced to see the movie in the company of our nine-year-old daughter. Although the latter had successfully absorbed the intellectual insults of several Ma and Pa Kettle films, she obviously felt that Hollywood had gone too far this time, and long before the end of the movie, we felt a hand tugging our sleeve in the darkness. We know now why the author of the best screenplay of 1956 failed to step up and receive his Oscar. Human dignity is not yet dead.

A clipping from *Publishers' Weekly* tells us, in time, we hope, to set up some sort of defense, that Eddie Cantor's book about his life is about to appear. The lives of George Jessel, Al Jolson, and Sophie Tucker all remind us that show people can make our lives sublime, if departing leave behind us, nothing in the sand of time. Mr. Cantor is calling his book *Take My Life,* and we feel that is an unfortunate suggestion. Or title.

Now we would like to say a few words about that lovable little urchin in the Italian movies—the utterly charming rascal who robs the American lady but in the final reel leads her back to her Italian lover and helps clear up their misunderstanding. Like other stock movie characters, he has been badly overworked and should be sent back to Central Casting for reassignment. The last time we saw him he had aged perceptibly and wasn't nearly as elfin as he used to be.

This is all, but it will help. And although we have written with the conviction of the truly indignant, we must exhort you not to lay too much store by this. After all, it's hot and like you, maybe we're just standing in the need of prayer.

DEFINING THE ISSUES, POINTING THE WAY, AND GUARDING THE GATE

It's none too soon to start thinking about next year's elections, and we are going to reproduce below the minutes of a ladies' club meeting which recently fell into our hands. Only the names, as the saying goes, are changed.

"The Tuesday Evening Club held its regular meeting last week at the home of Vice President Florence Davis with thirty members present. Senator Jasper A. Gooch, who is running for re-election, was the guest speaker, choosing as his subject 'Why My Opponent Is A Dangerous Man.'

"Senator Gooch said he wanted to quote some remarks of his opponent and then dissect them to show us what they really meant. In the first place, the Senator pointed out, his opponent had said he would help to balance the budget if elected. Senator Gooch explained that this was an open confession that his opponent wanted to tamper with our country's finances, and that the only way to prevent it was to vote for Gooch. The members applauded, showing that clubwomen can understand technical financial matters when properly presented.

"The Senator then quoted his opponent as saying he was in favor of our maintaining a strong Army and Navy. By using the word 'maintain' he is deliberately giving away vital military information to the enemy, Senator Gooch said, and this borders on treason. Mrs. Rawlings jumped up and made a motion that we write a letter to the editor of the newspaper, signing it The Tuesday Evening Club, asking Senator

Gooch's opponent to withdraw from the race in the best interests of the country. President Margaret O'Reilly asked her to defer the motion until the Senator had finished his speech.

"Senator Gooch then said his opponent had made a statement that if elected he wanted to help reduce the Federal payroll. That can mean only one thing, the Senator said, and that is that he wants centralized power in the hands of a few. In other words, Senator Gooch explained, he wants a dictatorship. Several members arose at the same time and there was some confusion as to who had the floor, but Mrs. Rawlings was finally recognized. She again made her motion, only this time she said the letter should be sent to the editor of *The New York Times* as well as to the local paper, and Secretary Madge Wilson seconded the motion. President O'Reilly said she was as badly frightened as anyone else at such statements, but asked again that the motion be held until the Senator had finished.

"Senator Gooch said he was only going to quote one more statement of his opponent's and that was that he would like to see us all working together for the common good. That's out and out Communist talk, the Senator said, adding that he would fight collectivism as long as he had the strength to.

"President O'Reilly had a hard time restoring order after that statement, but after thanking Senator Gooch for opening our eyes, she said Mrs. Rawlings' motion was in order. It passed unanimously.

Respectfully submitted,
The Secretary."

BORN ON THE WRONG SIDE OF THE SOUNDTRACKS

Well, it's been a disastrous year for television comedians, and we aren't surprised. For a long time now, the comedy programs have started us emptying the ashtrays and locking up for the night, and it's beginning to look as though we were not out of step. Some time ago—to be exact it was on a Sunday that Cleveland lost a game to the Yankees—Jack

Benny had a routine with a doctor in which the latter was trying to cure the comedian's laryngitis. It went like this:

> *Benny is stretched out on a couch with his mouth open, and the doctor (you knew he was a doctor because he had a reflector on his forehead) is peering intently down Benny's throat.*
> BENNY (anxiously): What are you looking for?
> DOCTOR (impishly): Cleveland's manager. He must be hiding somewhere.

Even the studio audience betrayed the sponsors on that one. There have been worse jokes, we imagine, but we haven't the steadiness required to mine the available material for one less appealing. So far as we can determine, it violated every known principle of humor, and we're surprised that the gag industry didn't know better. That brings up the question of what is known of humor, and we would like to say that, mysterious as it is, quite a lot is known of it. We have never seen on stage, screen, or television an operating room routine that was funny, and we seriously doubt that we ever will. To an extent this is true of courtroom routines; if the judge gets too drunk, or stupid, or hoydenish, we recoil, and the humor, if there was any, evaporates. What we are saying, perhaps, is that there are certain subjects with which humor cannot be associated, and if that is true we should drop the subjects.

The second serious error in the Benny gag was the fact that it was topical humor, which is the most fleeting, most evasive type of humor known. A newspaper headline is perishable enough, Lord knows, but the gag tied to it usually precedes the headline to the grave. A few years ago, E. B. White described his difficulties in putting together a humor anthology, and he expressed quite clearly what happens when some "terribly funny stories from the press" are collected. "We collected them, all right," he said, "and some of them were funny, too, but we soon had to keep them in a separate icebox on account of the way the cream was beginning to taste." The third error in the Benny gag lies in the utter incredibility of the situation. The Cleveland manager couldn't be hiding in Benny's throat, and nobody is imbecilic enough to think so.

A situation can be implausible, but not impossible. Groucho Marx was once invited to join a Hollywood club and he declined, saying "I don't care to belong to any club that would consider a man like me for membership." This is implausible behavior but we like to think it could happen and it amuses us. A situation can be exaggerated, distorted, and even twisted into pure nonsense, but it cannot be made incredible.

This may sound like a merciless dissection of a gag that's pretty terrible to begin with but it's only by working with the material at hand that we can see why television comedy is missing its mark. There's more to this analysis than prejudice, which is also present in a pure form. Many of the ingredients of humor have been identified, weighed, and clearly classified, and there's no reason why television gag writers should shut their eyes to the findings of their elders.

LAUGHING FIT TO CHILL

We've been trying for a long time to put our finger on exactly what's wrong with all of the various Weeks that promote doughnuts, or swim-for-health, or let's-eat-out, and now, after carefully reading a letter we received today, we think we know. There's no damn sense in them. The letter was from the Executive Director of the Twelfth Annual National Laugh Week (April 1–8, if you want to be getting yourself comfortable and clearing your throat), and its purpose was to sound us out to see if we cared to sponsor a Philadelphia contestant in the National Laugh Olympics, the purpose of which is "to promote the art of laughter." A set of instructions, accompanying the letter, good naturedly informed us that contestants should be tested for versatility, inventiveness, pacing, timing, and projection, and quoted Dick Coller, "Laff Champ of 1951," as saying there were 117 different kinds of laughs.

No, fellows, we don't want to sponsor a contestant. The only thing we sponsor is some charitable project which has managed to capture our imagination, such as the books we have written. But we're not going to let loose of your lapels yet because we have a few facts that we hope you don't laugh off. In the first place, laughter is not an art but a response, and unprovoked laughter is likely to be maniacal. The thought of a contestant laughing at nothing to demonstrate versatility, inventiveness, pacing, timing, and projection is enough to send a chill up our spine, and we can tell you now that his laugh would contain about the same heavy voltage of mirth as a fourth-grade Santa Claus shouting "Ho! Ho!" off-stage. We have heard people force a laugh, for some social or professional advantage, and in every case it was a bad moment all around. Humor is a tricky thing, depending, as it does, upon the kind of heart and mind the individual has, and the response to a humorous situation is equally unpredictable. We seldom laugh out loud, although we often enjoy what E. B. White calls "the inaudible, the enduring laugh," yet there was a point in the stage play *Mr. Roberts* where we cackled so hysterically that the manager had to turn on the house lights to restore us to normalcy. (We found out later that the orchestra was poised to go into "The Star Spangled Banner" if the lights hadn't worked.) But to laugh at nothing is a frightening thing, and we don't think any credit would accrue to us even if our man laughed and paced and timed his way to the top, and got to be the next Laff Champ. And so far as the various Weeks are concerned, don't bother us until National Phenobarbital Week comes around.

ARE YOU THE MAN I WAS TALKING TO LAST NIGHT'S BROTHER?

We would like to be a literary remora today, if you don't mind, and attach ourselves to a bigger fish, specifically Earl Wilson, the celebrated columnist. We strung along with Wilson when Frank Sinatra and Ava Gardner split up, and frankly, we couldn't have asked for a more complete record of the momentous day-to-day events. When, a short time later, Gloria Vanderbilt announced that she had Reached The End with Leopold Stokowski (we can't prevent some of the flavor of Wilson's style from seeping into these notes) we naturally turned to Wilson again, and, by George, there he was with everything the other columnists had, plus a few *exclusives* of his own. A loyalty such as we had built up for Wilson by this time isn't easily overturned, so when Rita Hayworth pinned the "Dear John" note to Dick Haymes's pillow and went into hiding, we sent out immediately for Wilson's column so we could see just what was really going on. But halfway through the column, our attention ground to a halt. We got no further than Wilson's statement that when Dick learned of Rita's flight "he almost cried real tears."

Now we've been working on that sentence, off and on, for two months, and we still haven't figured out what Wilson is trying to tell us. If he (Dick) had cried, the tears in this case would have been real, but he only *almost* cried; he didn't really shed any tears, real or otherwise. In other words, the tears that he did not shed were real tears. Is that it?

Well, before we had finished with Wilson, our eye was scanning an advertisement of the new Beverly Hilton Hotel in Hollywood, and we'll be damned if we didn't run into trouble again. Among the attractions listed, and it seemed to be a nifty layout all right, was "a sunken swimming pool." Now we've never heard of an elevated swimming pool or even a surface swimming pool, and we wonder if the copy writer was trying to put over some hidden meaning that we have innocently missed. Sooner or later—they've made great strides in geriatrics lately—we are going to get out to the Beverly Hilton and take a look at that pool. We would have done it this summer but for the fact that we were worn out from the reading we had been doing, and we decided to take a rest on a small island on the New Jersey coast. It was nice, too, with a sunken ocean (Atlantic) on one side and a sunken bay (Barnegat) on the other.

THE CUSTOMER'S ALL WET

It's hard to keep up with things, that's all we can say. No sooner do we get everything securely battened down here,

than trouble pops up there. The other day, just before checking out of a New York hotel, our eye was taken by a small
card lying on the telephone table. It read: "There is only one
satisfactory way to test a shower and that is to be under it.
It is obviously impractical for hotel employees to make this
test. Will you therefore be kind enough to comment in the
space below about the shower in this room, and leave the
card with the floor clerk? Thank you very much." Well, as
in the disintegration of our other freedoms, there are the ingredients for a fine little drama in this situation, and we are
pleased to give it an out-of-town tryout right now. Actors!
Lights! Curtain!

    *Scene: Hotel room. Guest is emptying closet and filling suit-
case. There is knock at the door.*

BELLBOY (*enters*): You sent for me?

GUEST: Yes, I'm checking out as soon as I get packed. Hand me
    those shoes.

BELLBOY (*passes shoes to Guest*): Of course you've filled out your
    shower card?

GUEST (*evasively*): Er—how's that?

BELLBOY (*doggedly*): Have you filled out your shower card?

GUEST (*lowering voice and glancing furtively toward door*): Look,
    I've been pretty busy this trip and I was wondering if I couldn't
    pass up the shower. You know—maybe catch it twice next time.

BELLBOY (*scathingly*): In other words, you'd skip without filling
    in your shower card? You're a jumper?

GUEST (*hanging head and scuffing rug*): It's just this once.

BELLBOY: That's the way it always starts. We let you off, and
    first thing you know you're skipping shower cards all over the
    country.

GUEST: How about you taking the shower for me? (*Quickly*) I'll
    make it worth your while.

BELLBOY: It is obviously impractical for hotel empl . . .

GUEST: I know, I know. (*Suddenly*) I've had a lot of experience
    with showers. I can tell just by turning it on whether or not
    it's okay.

BELLBOY (*closing eyes impatiently and reciting from memory*):
    There is only one satisfactory way to test a shower and that is
    to be under it.

GUEST (*defiantly*): I don't *have* to take a shower. I can tear up this card and just walk out.

BELLBOY: Does the hotel tell you it's got to be a hot shower or a cold shower? Does the hotel tell you it's got to be needle-spray or open-nozzle? No. I think you'll find the hotel has been more than reasonable.

GUEST (*abashed*): I'm sorry. I guess I lost my temper. (*Starts to bathroom*) I'll give it a try.

BELLBOY: That's the spirit. And just for that I'm going to recommend you for an Honor System Card.

GUEST (*pausing in door*): Honor System Card?

BELLBOY: That's right. Then when you check out we won't send the maid up to feel the shower curtain.

END

SEASONAL NOTE

We've never understood why the fashion magazines are always out of step where seasons are concerned. Their summer issues deal with furs and woolens, while their winter numbers feature shorts and cottons. The other day we picked up a fashion magazine and found the following statement which we would like to quote in its entirety:

"Those long, hot days are with us again and whether we like them or not there's nothing we can do until the tang in the air tells us autumn is here again. Our only relief from the heat is to dress appropriately. Milady will always be fresh and cool in cottons."

We glanced at the date on the magazine. It said March. Outside the snow was whipping past the window horizontally, and from the next room our wife was asking why we didn't go down the lane and help the mailman get unstuck. His truck had been in a drift for over an hour.

Knowing the Government dislikes outside intervention, we gave the mailman plenty of time to get out by himself, but he and his assistant were still at it when we walked up. The assistant was stamping his feet and blowing on his hands to keep warm.

"Howdy, Mr. McCullers," we said politely. The mailman looked up and grunted. "Those long, hot days are with us again," we said, trying to make conversation, "and whether we like it or not there's nothing we can do until the tang in the air tells us autumn is here again."

The mailman dropped his shovel and straightened up. The assistant stopped blowing on his hands.

"Yes sir," we went on, "our only relief from the heat is to dress appropriately."

The assistant moistened his lips nervously and looked searchingly at the mailman. Neither spoke.

"I guess Mrs. McCullers keeps fresh and cool in her cottons, doesn't she?" we asked the mailman.

We didn't see the signal, but since they both leaped at once we knew some motion was made.

"The crazier they are the more they struggle," the mailman said. "Try not to hurt him because he doesn't know what he's doing."

Well, maybe not, maybe not. But neither did that fashion editor.

ARTS AND LETTERS

If we ever write a book—which is very unlikely since we've never climbed Mt. Everest, never been a communist, and never had any views on the power of positive thinking— it will be a fairly petulant volume on the present compulsive drive of modern artists and writers, especially poets, toward obscurantism. We used to think—we were all young once— that the responsibility of the poet or artist was to communicate; now, we know better. His function is *not* to communicate. Lord knows we try to be as cultural as the next man and when we first read that Dylan Thomas' poem we tried to look knowledgeable and pleased, but honestly we didn't get anything out of it that we could take home. Ezra Pound and James Joyce baffle us even more, although we must say that the presence of Pound's *Pisan Cantos* on the coffee table has brought us more respect than anything we can imagine, short of referring to the late John Foster Dulles as Jack.

What we're leading up to is a confession that we broke up an art reception recently by criticizing the abstract work of one of the artists. We say this reluctantly because the affair does us no credit. It was a pleasant gathering, one of those summer afternoon parties following the opening of a new exhibition, where the gentle murmur of conversation is broken occasionally by a low laugh—an art reception-type laugh. We had asked one of the artists why it was that every painting in the exhibition except one was abstract, and without waiting for his reply we ventured the opinion that the answer lay in the fact that modern artists were lazy. In painting abstracts, we said, warming to a subject we knew very little about, the artist runs less risk of being shown up as a person of little talent, since he could always silence critics with the claim that the point of his painting had been missed. In other words, the burden of defense had shifted. The critic must prove that he is *qualified* to look at the painting. We were vaguely aware of the silence which had fallen over the group, but we had miscalculated badly the amount of criticism modern artists can absorb. The artist to whom we had been talking, placed his drink on the nearest table and marched stiffly from the room, followed a few moments later by his admirers.

Well, if a man is to be measured by the adversaries he takes on, we would like to say the artist exited grandly, his plume high, his head erect. But he didn't. Instead of a panache flowing in the wind, we got the distinct impression as he left the room that one of the propellers of his beanie was feathered.

HANDS ACROSS THE SEA

We buttonholed you a few months ago and gave you our views on modern poetry, abstract art, James Joyce, and what we felt was the compulsive drive of modern artists and writers toward obscurantism. You may recall that we went even further and described an art reception that we had attended last summer in Maine, at which this subject was treated. The discussion there over abstract painting, at the time we joined it, had descended precipitously into accusation and personal abuse, and on this level we felt qualified to join in. After we had addressed a few remarks on the subject, the leading artist, an abstractionist, departed abruptly, leaving half of his Martini in the glass.

The response to the essay was neither disappointing nor gratifying; a New York newspaper reprinted part of it, a lady from Pittsburgh wrote us a note that said "Cheers!" (nothing obscure about her feeling), and The Pennsylvania Academy of the Fine Arts sent us an invitation to join (sly as it was, there was nothing obscure about *that*, either). Well, we were pleased at having had our say and we were going to let it go at that when suddenly a new and powerful ally showed up and joined hands with us. Our new friend is Lord Dunsany, the Irish poet and dramatist, who arrived in New York recently for a lecture tour and promptly gave the shipboard reporters his views on modern poetry. "It's muck," he said.

"Clarity is the first duty of poets," Lord Dunsany said, taking the words right out of our mouth, "and in looking at today's poetry one should realize symbols aren't any good if they aren't clear. This stuff that is called modern verse ought to have a court of appeals to judge what it really is." Excited by the scent of blood, we started searching quickly through the newspaper account of Lord Dunsany's remarks hoping we would encounter the names of Dylan Thomas ("Altarwise in the owl-light at the half-way house"), or Ezra Pound ("He had moved amid her phantasmagoria, amid her galaxies, NUKTIS 'AGALMA"), or Gertrude Stein ("There is a way to see in onion and surely very surely rhubarb and a tomato, surely very surely there is that seeding"—Note to the proofreader: We don't care what you think, set it the way we've got it), but there were no names. "It's just muck," he repeated, "and people ought to be honest. When they don't understand it, they should say they don't. They seem to fear being considered ignorant if they dislike it."

Thank you, Lord Dunsany. You're as dainty as a bulldozer.

PRESS RELEASE

We keep an eye out for unusual press releases, convinced beyond doubt that some of today's greatest literature is distributed for immediate release. Well, we unearthed a deposit the other day—to use a handy figure of speech—that struck us as being as rich as anything previously uncovered in this line. It follows:

"Potential producers of forthcoming Broadway productions have just been notified of a sure way in which to cut down overhead and expenses.

"The Zion Kosher Meat Company has offered, regardless of the status of advance sales or magnitude of the stars, to furnish free of charge all props pertaining to salami, baloney, liverwurst, corned beef, pastrami, etc., in edible or display form depending upon the nature of the particular scene.

"The Zion people feel that this dynamic invitation should be a boon to producers and should result in many more theatrical ventures for the forthcoming season."

2

Man *vs.* The System

GOOD LUCK, MISS HUNTER!

One of the truly great news stories of the year, in our opinion, has occurred in Manchester, England, and we regret that it was largely ignored by the American press. The event—nothing more or less than the continued unfolding of the human struggle against the machines man has created —concerned the failure of Margaret Hunter, a sixty-four-year-old Manchester lady, to pass her driving test. A Manchester newspaper, reporting the story crisply, declared that Miss Hunter had been taking driving lessons for twenty-five years, but that "she flunked her driving test again today, *as expected.*"

Miss Hunter, pictured as a frail, white-haired school teacher, took the test against a background of unsettling events which included a collision, the creation of a monstrous traffic jam, and the cowardly resignation of a driving instructor who was described as "having fled for his life." It would have unnerved anyone.

According to the Manchester report, Miss Hunter set out

from her home town of Stockport with a friend in a borrowed car and took the test at Manchester's Withington driving-test branch. After thirty minutes at the controls, she surrendered. "But the car is not damaged," she pointed out triumphantly as she descended.

"I thought I had done quite well," Miss Hunter told reporters later, "but actually I didn't expect to pass. I shall take the test again when I have had a little more practice." It was then that Miss Hunter revealed that she had been taking instructions for twenty-five years, and implied that one couldn't expect results overnight.

The Manchester newspaper suspected that Miss Hunter's test was a possible news event when, a few days earlier, her instructor had leaped from the car crying, "This is suicide." The following day she took her car for a practice spin but got only one hundred yards before she collided with a truck. On the day preceding her test, she hunted up another instructor—a man named Robert Tongue, who had few dependents—and took the car on the highway again. When she finally pulled off onto a side road, she had twenty miles of snarled traffic behind her.

That lesson, her forty-second, left her full of confidence, and she asked permission to take the test.

"I've not looked at the form to see why I failed," Miss Hunter said after it was all over. "My thumb was sore from the accident, and I was not used to changing gears or starting the car. But I'm pleased to see that someone had enough confidence in me to allow me to use it. I'm quite confident now."

Mr. Tongue was somewhat less optimistic. He said he didn't care to be drawn into a discussion of whether or not he would continue as Miss Hunter's instructor. Friends felt that Mr. Tongue had aged.

Miss Hunter will be back next month for another test, and she has our best wishes all the way.

TRY THE OTHER CHANNEL

Television humor (*tel'e·vizh'un hu'mer, n.,* of, or pertaining to, a humorous situation in which the comic element is telegraphed ahead in sufficient time for young and old alike to get it) has now spread to books, and, to take a cowardly attitude, we're sorry that we lived to see it. We had no trouble passing over the terribly cute Art Linkletter and Groucho Marx works—they were acknowledged projections of the authors' television endeavors—but now we have at hand a trio of volumes that have no *apparent* ancestral ties to the small screen but whose texts instantly establish the kinship. All three lack, almost totally, the comic or humorous gift, and we doubt if three sillier books could be found anywhere. We propose to discuss them here because they seem to offer a warning as to what we may expect when television humor escapes from the screen.

How to Write Ten Different Best Sellers Now in Your Spare Time and Become the First Author on Your Block Unless There's an Author Already Living on Your Block in Which Case You'll Become the Second Author on Your Block and That's Okay Too and Other Stories, by George Kirgo (Simon & Schuster) is fully as bad as the title implies. "Suppose your spirits are low," Kirgo writes. "You're down in the dumps. Write a letter to a distant friend and pretend you're the seven-cent airmail stamp. The minute you lick it, your spirits will soar." Now, do you believe us?

Moving on to *Which Way to Mecca, Jack?* by William Peter Blatty (Bernard Geis Associates), we come to a book the first line of which reads: "My mother is an Arab, which would make me half Arab, except that my father was an Arab too." The temptation to halt at that point we found irresistible. However, if you wish to know more about the author, we refer you to the following excerpt from the biographical sketch on the dust jacket: "Get him (Blatty) drunk on Horlick's malted-milk balls and he'll even claim that, as a Georgetown undergraduate, he kidnaped the Villanova wildcat while posing as an Augustinian priest." The sketch ends with this sentence: "Good *grief,* what a character!" Yes.

In *How to Run a Million into a Shoestring, and Other Shortcuts to Success* by Carl Winston (Putnam), every possible joke can be identified long before it crosses the horizon. The first chapter, "Life Begins at Birth," should, but doesn't quite prepare you for: "Ten Rules for Successful Failure," "How to Take the Work out of Sex," "Live a Year in 183 Days," and "Why You're Overweight, Underweight, or Both." The publishers, unwilling to let the good humor stop, offer on the back cover, as a prize for the best reader's quote, "two complimentary shoestrings, autographed by the author."

This sort of thing could drive us back into the arms of Max Shulman.

TAKE TWO ASPIRIN
AND TUNE IN TOMORROW

Dr. Ben Casey and Dr. Kildare are "practicing good medicine," we are advised by a press release from the American Medical Association.

Well, the body of medical knowledge is growing these days at a rate greater than our capacity to worry about it, but an announcement like that can bring us in on Saturday and Sunday for a little overtime worrying. We have suspected for some time that the AMA's interest in medical problems was a bit more political than scientific, but we were still startled to learn that it could take its eye off the ball for a reason no more compelling than to give its blessing—like Duncan Hines knighting a tearoom—to some television soap operas.

The AMA quotes its own Physicians Advisory Committee on Radio, Television, and Motion Pictures, as saying, "The dedication to the profession and the sincere personal interest in the patients exhibited by the residents and interns on the Casey and Kildare shows, their financial plight, and their inner workings have given the public an accurate picture of the long, tough struggle to become a practicing physician." The more we contemplate that statement, the more we are aware of some inner workings within us. Many doctors work hard and under circumstances of great tension, but the

AMA doesn't touch us when they seek to bring tears to our
eyes because of the financial plight of the profession. As a
patient, we've had our wallet fluoroscoped too often. And it
was just a few months ago that the AMA helped bring about
defeat of the Medicare bill—for better or worse—with a Greek
chorus of doctors in the background muttering threats of a
strike if the bill passed. We still don't see how it's possible
to strike against a government medical system without also
striking against sick and dying patients, but we assume this
will all be explained in due time by either Casey or Kildare.

What surprised us as much as anything was not so much
the knowledge of the existence of the AMA's Advisory Committee but rather the clumsy manner in which the workings
of the committee were revealed. According to the AMA, the
committee checks scripts before they are put into production
and while usually only minor changes need to be made, sometimes scripts "are rejected altogether." We can see it clearly,
this exercise in applied nostalgics: the rain beating down,
the buggy wheels grinding through the mud, the kindly old
doctor walking by lantern light to the kitchen door. A half-
hour later he is plodding back to the buggy, the newborn
baby's cries can be heard faintly from an upstairs bedroom,
and he is tucking a few bills into his waistcoat pocket. "Cut!"
shouts the director. "That money-folding scene has to go.
That's no way to depict the financial plight of the physician.
I couldn't face the AMA committee with such an unrealistic
picture of the medical profession as that."

The feeling that doctors are somehow sacred seems to be
so firmly fixed in our national guilt complex that we hardly
know how to present what follows. But a few day ago we were
idling through the August 20 issue of *Modern Medicine*
("The Magazine of Diagnosis and Treatment") and we
came across a paragraph that said during the first half of 1962
medical care prices continued to rise more than twice as
much as prices in general. "Higher professional fees and
higher rates for hospital rooms and health insurance spurred
the advance," the article said. Well, now that the evenings

are darkening quickly, there'll be more time for television, and we doubt there's a problem here that can't be solved on one channel or another, but the usual box-office carpentry won't do it. Now that our suspicions are aroused we're going to examine every show from "Mister Ed," the talking horse, to—oh my God, they wouldn't, would they?

CAN YOU SAY IT IN ENGLISH?

English is one of the oldest and most satisfying of languages, and we would like to ask if anyone—any adult in his right mind—really believes that the mutilation of the language by various professional groups is making it any easier, any more facile, or any more expressive? A few days ago we picked up a book from a friend's coffee table (we're an incurable book browser, and would leaf through the city directory of Shreveport, Louisiana, if nothing more brilliant were available) and came upon the following startling sentence:

> "The theory of automata is relevant to behavioral science in the sense that it is an absolutely rigorous theory of processes which are themselves absolutely rigorous abstractions of behavior."

We glanced at the outside of the book and found it a handsome volume that certainly did credit to the publisher if not the author. We read the sentence again, wondering if we were losing our mind, then closed the book and returned it to the coffee table. We can handle a simple infraction of grammar, such as "Are you the man I was walking down the street with last night's brother?" but the theory of automata is the mystery to us now that it always was.

This experience should have prepared us for what lay in store, but it didn't. Picking up a quarterly magazine recently, one of those highly authoritarian little publications that we always suspect of beaming something insidious at us on a subliminal level, we read: "*Behavioral Science* and the *Journal of Conflict Resolution* each produced a special issue relating to game theory as their first issues of 1962. This issue includes articles which discuss the applications of game-theory concepts and empirical results to problems of individual and group behavior in social-conflict situations." We know what they mean by 1962, but that's the limit of our comprehension in that sentence.

Not long ago we received a letter from a student at Columbia University asking our advice on a writing enterprise he had undertaken. He began his letter by asking if he could outline his "methodology." We wrote a fairly cross letter in reply, in which we quoted E. B. White's belief on the subject: ". . . there simply is a better chance of doing well if the writer holds a steady course, enters the stream of English quietly, and does not thrash about." "Methodology" is thrashing about.

Don't think we're against expressive or colorful writing, because we are not. We treasure still a letter received over a year ago from a young daughter to whom we had made a gift of an album of three records. The album was to replace one that was incomplete. "I still had one record," the letter said clearly and beautifully, "but I was glad to get a whole nother set."

ADAMS' RIB

We have never ceased to be astonished at the durability of that subdivision of the entertainment business known as the gag industry; the assembly lines roll endlessly, the products are uniform (not of good quality, necessarily, but uniform), and the packaging and distribution must certainly be the envy of Marshall Field's. For hours we have sat and mused—brooded, really—over the genesis of a gag: who started it, how, and why? Well, we think we know now, or at least we know more about it than we did.

A few days ago we were reading Earl Wilson's column (an important unit in the distribution system, incidentally) and one gag rang a bell in our memory. It was a plangent clangor, really, because the story turned out to be a retreaded version of the story of Hugh Best and the elephant shells. "Comedian

Joey Adams," Wilson wrote, "tells of a man who went into Hammacher Schlemmer's and ordered 9,000 elephant-gun cartridges. 'But 9,000!' exclaimed a salesman. 'What are you going to do with 9,000?' The customer explained, 'Well, you see, I just don't like elephants.' "

As we see it, Adams is guilty of not one but two offenses: he stole the gag in the first place, and he ruined it in the second. The trade assures us that no knavery is involved in the theft of gags (a moral issue is involved here which may be a little too subtle for the studio audience), but to tell a good story in such a way as to have it lie there like a rare old Axminster—a comedian is answerable to that, all right. The single factor working in Adams' behalf is our realization that the life of a comedian is a precarious one. The careers of most comedians have been on the rocks more often than Scotch whisky—to steal a gag from a comedian we'll be damned if we will identify.

WE SUPPOSE IT HAS SOME INTEREST AS AN ANTIQUE

We guess it all depends upon which side of the cash register you're standing on as to what kind of treatment you get from a used-car dealer. If you're buying a car, the model sitting there is a sweet-running machine that was used only by a little old lady who drove out to the country once a year to buy herself a Christmas tree. If it's something you've brought in for a trade-in, the dealer looks at it as if it were something that couldn't qualify for an inspection sticker even in Tijuana.

The other day we rolled up to the showroom of a new-car dealer in a car that had left there so recently it still had lint from the carpet on it. The dealer eyed it with distaste.

"I'm sorry you turned the ignition off," he said. "The tow truck is out on a call and—"

"Don't worry about that," we said cheerfully. "It'll start if I snap my fingers. I brought it around for an appraisal."

The dealer shot me a glance that was freighted with all of

the warmth he would have shown a Collector of Internal Revenue.

"Has it been turned down for scrap iron?" he asked.

We laughed, but it was a unilateral action. "Anybody who would turn in a car this good should have a net thrown over him," we said. "It's just that I like the new model and thought that if you'd give me the right kind of deal—"

The dealer walked around the car, looking puzzled. "I don't remember when they made this model," he said. "Of course, I'm only forty-nine."

We were getting nettled. "Look, friend," we said, "you sold me this car less than a year ago and there's—"

He held up his hand. "What does it burn?" he asked. "Gasoline?"

"No," we snapped. "Cooking sherry."

He ignored me and circled the car again. "I guess you've completed your payments anyway," he said. "You couldn't still owe anything—"

"Are you going to make me an offer on this car?" we asked tartly.

"Yes," he said. "Leave it here and I won't charge you for parking."

We laughed mirthlessly. "You've got to do better than that."

"One final offer," he said. "No parking charge and you can make one local telephone call. Take it or leave it."

We called home and said we had bought a new car.

LOOK BACK IN LANGUOR

A friend of ours who may or may not know such things (you never question the source of these utterances) just told us that the passenger seats in jet planes cost nearly two thousand dollars each, and this knowledge has plunged us into a midsummer angst. We think it's a shame that the airlines should go to so much trouble to make their passengers comfortable and then be betrayed by a game played by some of them. The rules of this game, as nearly as we can determine by observation, go something like this:

Exercise 1.   Wait until the passenger behind you has started reading a magazine, then punch your seat button and lower yourself into his lap. If properly worked, this will telescope the magazine against his knees and he won't be able to get at it until the plane lands.

Exercise 2.   If this little drama is enacted when the rear passenger has a tray of food in front of him, it will alter his plans somewhat at point of destination. (We saw this happen to a lady once, between New York and Miami, and we still wonder where she went when she got off the plane. We must admit we laughed when it happened—it was the gravy on her eyeglasses that startled us—but we stopped quickly when we saw the look in her eyes.)

Exercise 3.   The greatest menace is the passenger pulling the Pearl Harbor or surprise attack. He waits until the man behind him has asked for a second cup of coffee. Then, when the coffee is still at maximum temperature, he leans back hard and pushes the button.

Exercise 4.   The most pathetic case we ever witnessed personally was on a flight to Chicago when the man sitting beside us lifted an attaché case to his knees and began groping inside for some papers. At that moment, the passenger in front of him pushed the button for full release. The pilot said later it was the first sound from the cabin he had ever heard over the noise of a jet engine.

YOU WANT TO KNOW
WHO I'M VOTING FOR?

It was only a few days ago that we were sitting here, drumming our fingers on the desk top (we were employing a sort of arpeggio since we learned that the man in the next office had less of a tolerance for this than for any other movement) and wondering why it was that no poll takers had ever sought our opinion on any subject. "Public-opinion polls reach everyone in America from the farmer in his field right up to the President of the United States, Thomas E. Dewey," Goodman Ace once remarked. But somehow we were always overlooked. Then suddenly it happened. As we were coming out of an airline office on Fifth Avenue, a lady forced a card into our hand and inquired if we recognized the names of any of the planes printed there. She held a clip board in the crook of one arm, and there was a resolute expression on her face that suggested she would brook no nonsense. She had the manner of a woman who worked *The New York Times* crossword puzzle in ink. We held the card out at arm's length, to accommodate a minor visual flaw having nothing to do with age, and glanced at the names.

"All of these names are familiar to me," we said, glancing up, "but I don't see anything about Nixon or Kennedy. Don't you want to know—"

"Is there any one plane listed here that you would refuse to ride in?" she asked, checking a form held to the clip board.

"No," we said, "I would ride in any of them. But if you want to know which plane I would prefer for Nixon to ride in, then I think I'd say—"

"How many flights have you taken during the year just ended?" she asked.

"Ten or twelve," we replied dispiritedly. "Don't you want to know about our 3.4 children or our median income of—?"

"All domestic flights?"

We answered affirmatively. "I own 1.8 automobiles," we offered hopefully, "which projected on a—"

"Had you rather ride in jet planes than in piston aircraft?"

"Can you list me as undecided?" we asked, pleased at the chance to show that we knew our way around the categories. "And if the election were being held today, my vote would—"

"One final question," she said, her pen poised over the clip board. "For ground transportation, how much more often do you use limousines than taxis?"

"That's a comparison," we said, "and it needs clarification. Do you mean by geographic region? By marital status? By size of household? By occupation status? By socioeconomic group? By sex? By age? By education—aged ten and over? By home ownership? By metropolitan—"

She took the card from our hand and turned away. "Wait a minute," we said. "You didn't mention provisions for variable stability and control characteristics. What about qualitative ratings? Conceptual measurements? It isn't fair to just ask a few questions and wander off."

But she had already handed the card to another man. Oh well, it wasn't what we dreamed it would be, but we were polled anyway.

LET ME HAVE THAT TROWEL, MAYOR

Ambivalence is a very fashionable word right now—it has completely displaced dichotomy which was riding high just a year ago—and when a word is fashionable we won't use it. But there isn't a better word to describe our feeling about the name-changing that's going on; we are fascinated by the absurdity of it and at the same time dismayed at its total impracticality. Take, for example, the Avenue of the Americas, a thoroughfare that to us and to just about everybody we know is Sixth Avenue. We've never had the nerve to tell a cab driver to deliver us to the Avenue of the Americas, but we've got a pretty good idea of what he would say, and that has restrained us. Just what persuaded the late Mayor La-Guardia to switch the names is a frustrating puzzle, but it shows that he could produce something pretty terrible when he put his mind to it.

Several years ago someone in the Pennsylvania state government reasoned that it would be a handsome thing to do to name one of the state highways after a Mr. Joseph W. Hunter who had once served as the state's highway commissioner. Since no new highways were available for christening, the state declared that the Bethlehem Pike would henceforth be known as the Joseph W. Hunter Highway. Only it hasn't been. The highway still extends to Bethlehem, it is still known as the Bethlehem Pike, and if you call it anything else you will be looked at curiously. On the outskirts of Philadelphia, where the highway begins, there is a sign proclaiming the road to be the Joseph W. Hunter Highway, but even the sign has a defeated look about it.

It's a national characteristic for Americans to shorten names (viz., the alphabetical agencies in Washington), so it would appear that the namers are asking for trouble when they christen a building the George Caldwell O'Halloran Memorial Nurses Residential Hall and Recreational Center. It's already been shortened to "the dorm" before the girls even move in. In our college, a small but venerable Virginia institution, we recall a building called the George Preston Blow, Jr. Memorial Gymnasium. As you've already guessed, this was called "the gym" and if any of the students had called it anything different he would likely have had a net thrown over him.

All of these, of course, are demonstrations of local nonsense, but they lead us to that monument of national absurdity which is Boulder Dam or Hoover Dam, depending upon your political conviction. According to the Democrats the proper name is Boulder Dam, but this is hotly disputed by the Republicans who claim that this name was conceived as a slight to the former president and that the true name of the reclamation project is Hoover Dam. Although the truth—if such exists—has been obscured by the swirling mists of political demagoguery, maps, road signs, post cards, and cane pennants have been produced in about equal number, with the result that an easy solution to the matter now may be beyond our reach. One suggestion that has been made is that the former president change his name to Herbert Boulder. It may be the only way out.

WAS THAT ACCIDENT ACCIDENTAL?

There was a time, not many years ago, when if you clipped another car accidentally you sheepishly admitted your guilt and invited the other owner to drive his car around to your garage and have the crumpled fender straightened.

"Tell Mac to put it on my bill," you would say, after which you would shake hands warmly and part friends. But no more.

A few days ago the front bumper of our car touched the rear bumper of the car ahead of me. It was a gentle tap, like two billiard balls coming together, so we were surprised to see the driver of the other car get out quickly and start bawling for help. We lowered our window. "What's the matter with you?" we inquired politely.

"I'm bleeding to death," he said. "Get me to a hospital."

"There's no broken glass," we said. "You couldn't be bleeding."

He grasped himself in the midriff. "It's internal," he said, his voice lowering to a hoarse croak. "Get me help. Quick."

We got out of our car to get a better look. "There's been no collision," we said. "The cars barely touched. There's not a scratch on either."

He let his hands fall. "You're insured, aren't you?" he asked suspiciously. We said that we were, but invited him to look at his car and see for himself it was undamaged.

"If I could only turn my head," he said, "I'd like to see what's left of it." He struggled to move his head with both hands. "I think my neck's broken. How much you carrying, five and ten?"

A woman was sitting in the front seat of the other car and we directed an appeal to her. "There's been no accident here," we said, "has there?"

The man let go of his head and limped quickly to the door. "She can't answer," he said. "She's in shock." He rubbed his thigh gingerly. "Just as I thought, a compound fracture. I'll be lucky if I get back to work in three months."

We got in our car and started the motor. "Pull up a little," we commanded. "I want to get by."

He looked surprised. "It won't move," he said. "It's a total loss."

We backed up and pulled around him, forcing him to jump nimbly to the side. "Send me a tow car," he shouted as we drove away, "and an ambulance, and the forms to fill out—"

THE PLOUGH AND THE STARS
(DOMESTIC VERSION)

Well, we see that censorship is back with us again, accompanied, as it often is, by a distrust of something called "intellectualism." A recent issue of *Variety* carried a total of thirty-three news stories dealing with censorship in the entertainment field; twice last week workmen in Times Square went aloft to paint more clothes on the lady in the advertisement for the motion picture *The Naked Maja;* customs officials are studying the criteria to be used in determining the "seriousness" of the scholars who wish to acquire copies of Henry Miller's *The Tropic of Capricorn;* and Philadelphia police recently raided several mid-town coffeehouses accused of being the hangout of "intellectuals and other shady characters." (The Philadelphia Police Department has 676 motor vehicles and last year they were involved in 734 accidents, more than two a day, but that's neither here nor there.)

There's the framework here for a fine inflammatory drama, in the tradition of Sean O'Casey, Frank O'Connor, and Liam O'Flaherty, and if someone would dim the house lights and give us a few bars of "The Rose of Tralee," we will commence.

Scene: A Philadelphia coffeehouse in the late afternoon. At curtain a young man is seated at a table, reading a book and stirring his coffee. Another young man enters quickly, glances furtively around, and sits at the table.

SECOND YOUTH (*breathlessly*): That was a close call. A squad car pulled up just as I got to the door. But it turned out they were raiding a drugstore in the next block.

FIRST YOUTH: Drugstore?

SECOND YOUTH (*nodding*): There's a newsstand there that sells the *London Economist* and the *Paris Review.* Cops have been watching the customers from a building across the street for two weeks. I was tipped off.

FIRST YOUTH: So was I. A fellow I know, whose brother is a cop, smuggled me out some aspirin.

SECOND YOUTH (*gazing with horror-stricken expression at friend's book*): That—that book—are you crazy?

FIRST YOUTH: It's *Swann's Way* by Marcel Proust. Did you think it was something by Henry Miller?

SECOND YOUTH (*looking anxiously around and lowering voice*): But Proust! He's intellectual as hell. What are you trying to do—get the place knocked over?

FIRST YOUTH: I never thought of Proust that way, but I guess you're right. (*Closes book and tries to shove it in trench coat pocket but it apparently collides with another object. He removes a crumpled theater program.*)

SECOND YOUTH (*freezing*): My God, *Le Ballet Africain!* Even in New York the license commissioner made them put on more clothes—

FIRST YOUTH (*now worried*): Yes, I know. I should have thrown it away. (*Looks around for a hiding place.*) Maybe I can conceal it in the back of my Tolstoy's *The Kreutzer Sonata.* (*Removes volume from other pocket.*)

SECOND YOUTH (*blanching*): Are you insane? Taking that book out in plain daylight, just as though it were *Tarzan of the Apes.* (*A police siren is heard dimly in the distance.*)

FIRST YOUTH (*beginning to break*): I've been thrown out of two coffeehouses already for being a shady character. If I'm caught here, I'm finished. (*The siren sounds closer.*)

SECOND YOUTH (*quickly*): Then you have nothing to lose. Here, take this. (*Removes a book from his pocket and thrusts it into hands of friend.*) My whole life is ahead of me.

FIRST YOUTH (*reading title aloud*): *The Life of Goya.* (*Sound of siren swells and suddenly stops.*) Not the story on which—

SECOND YOUTH:—*The Naked Maja* is based? The very same. (*Starts for window.*) Good luck. (*Disappears.*) (*The door gives way to axes and police enter. First youth is slowly tearing up his library card, but suddenly realizes he is caught with too much evidence and sinks into chair as curtain falls.*)

ONLY IN AMERICA

CHAIRMAN (*banging gavel*): The Civil Service Review Board is now in session. What is the charge against this defendant?

INVESTIGATOR (seats government worker on witness stand): He refuses to use the approved forms of expression.

CHAIRMAN (*peering over glasses*): Perhaps he's just ignorant.

INVESTIGATOR (*laughs hollowly*): There's no one in government so ignorant he doesn't know better than to say "pass along" when he means "channelize." Furthermore, on one occasion he wrote "general situation" instead of "overall picture."

CHAIRMAN (*shocked*): This is serious. Do you have any documents? (*coughs apologetically*) I mean documentary support?

INVESTIGATOR: There is an abundance of supporting data, which will be submitted in quintuplicate. That reminds me the defendant has been heard—in the cafeteria and other public places—substituting the word "information" for "data."

CHAIRMAN (*sternly*): Is this true?

DEFENDANT (*hanging head*): I didn't mean to use the—

INVESTIGATOR (*sharply*): Utilize.

DEFENDANT: Utilize the wrong term. I was worried about—

INVESTIGATOR: Concerned with—

DEFENDANT: I was concerned with the safety of the information and—

INVESTIGATOR: He means security of the data.

DEFENDANT: That's right. I didn't want certain letters to—

INVESTIGATOR: Certain correspondence.

DEFENDANT: Certain correspondence to be seen by other employees—

INVESTIGATOR (*wearily*): Other *personnel,* please.

DEFENDANT: Other personnel before I could put it in the files. So I—

INVESTIGATOR (*translating*): He means integrate it with the files. Mr. Chairman, this man is so obviously unfit to serve the government that continuation of this hearing is merely a regularization and formalization (*Savors terms*) Regularization and formalization.

CHAIRMAN: Have you anything to say before I—

INVESTIGATOR: Excuse me, Mr. Chairman, but you must mean "prior to." After all, "before" hasn't been used since prior to the Coolidge Administration.

CHAIRMAN (*flushing*): Of course. The defendant has me making errors. I find him guilty and the punishment is termination by —by—(*He looks hopefully at Investigator*).

INVESTIGATOR (*quickly*): Involuntary separation for cause, fully supported by documentation and concurrence of principal supervisory personnel.

CHAIRMAN (*nods appreciatively*): Thank you.

Gavel Falls

DELUXE MODEL

Overheard at a filling station, where an attendant was refueling a chauffeur-driven limousine: "Better shut off your engine. You're gaining on me."

WE WANT TO HEAR WHAT
WE HAVE TO SAY

Our Washington man reports that the House Commission on Government Reorganization has been turned down in its request for a copy of its own report. The State Department has stamped it "Secret."

SUPER COLOSSAL

Recently, we've been troubled by the decline of the newsreel, and we've been putting some thought into means of bringing about its revival. Our best idea so far, and, mind you, we're just thinking out loud, is the production of a newsreel epic which would demonstrate what the inventive genius of the motion-picture world can produce when unselfishly pooled. To get the producers thinking along the right lines, we are offering the following crude scenario. It covers the most dramatic moments likely to occur in a given year, but, if necessary, it could be expanded. Perhaps a real news shot could be added, but we personally are against it. This is hardly the time for experimentation.

SCENE I

This is a ski scene which shows a covey of skiers hurtling down a mountainside. The sound track man says: "Yessir, folks, this is really the sport of thrills. Thrills and . . . oops, SPILLS! But it's all part of the sport so who cares?"

(Close-up of the man who fell down. His lips form a very short sentence which quite properly is cut out of the sound track.)

Scene II

This scene shows a man and a woman water skiing behind a speedboat at Cypress Gardens, Florida. "It may look easy," the sound man says, "but for sheer skill and excitement there's nothing like a run on the water skis. Look out, lady, you're in for a ducking!"

(Close-up of the lady, who seems to be making precisely the same comment as the skier. She has not only ruined her permanent but is also getting ready to go down for the third time.)

Scene III

This is a stadium scene at a football game. The camera moves across the faces of the crowd and picks out a large woman who is clearly registering disgust at the way things are going.

(Close-up shows that her program is for the dog show at Madison Square Garden. Some people disgust easily.)

Scene IV

This is a fashion scene. A woman announcer says: "Milady will wear lettuce and other vegetables on her head this spring. . . ." A model wearing a fixed smile and a headpiece of fresh garden vegetables slowly turns her head toward the camera. The announcer says, "If we just had some mayonnaise now. . . ."

(The model raises one hand to her head and her fingers curl menacingly around a tomato.)

Scene V

This is the diving scene where a man dives off the high board and the shot is reversed, making him leap from the water back to the board. (A terrific scene and one that every red-blooded newsreel fan will insist on.)

This scenario isn't as crude as I thought. Is there an Academy Award for newsreels?

ON THE BEACH

For a long time (too long, it now appears) we watched with strained tolerance the struggle between men and women which, in retrospect, seems to have left the cold-war stage right after World War II. For a while it was fun to watch, the women being absurdly arrogant as they got a better grip on their authority and the men being petulant as they discovered no one was impressed any longer with their Clarence Day attitudes, when suddenly the laughter left and the whole thing took on a life-and-death character. We used to think one of our finest moments was to lean an arm on a mantelpiece, swirl the olive in our glass, and tell our fellow dinner guests—in a first-rate Peter DeVries manner—how we felt about the thing: "In the war between the sexes," we would say owlishly, "we are a conscientious objector." It was a good line, all right, but we don't say it any more, for the same reason, perhaps, that Chamberlain suddenly stopped saying that all Hitler wanted to do was to take back the Fatherland. One day Man was the stronger sex, the next day he was just bewildered, groping through the reference books to see where nature, God, and his own philosophers had let him down.

In the first flush of their victory, the Women were generous. All they wanted was Equality, they said, nothing more. When they reached that point, though, they didn't pause long enough to touch up their lipstick. Oh, some things that were well established could go on, the victors said. Men could continue to die younger than women, the incidence of widowhood could continue its ascent, construction work and stoop-labor could remain the right of man, and, if they wanted to, they could continue to paint the greatest pictures, write the greatest books, compose the greatest symphonies, and think the loftiest thoughts. None of that would be disturbed, they promised, if man recognized his place and kept in it. Any student of history knew this couldn't work; the victor can't grant the vanquished equality. It didn't work, and Women soon dropped the pretense.

Well, we've brooded about this a good bit, along with some other poor losers, and we're willing to concede the battle lost but hope something can be salvaged from the reconstruction period that lies ahead. To that end, we've been reading the works of our leading traitors—D. H. Lawrence, Ashley Montagu, and others who have supported Woman in her belief that she must control the world. From our reading has come a sort of pleasant confusion—exactly the kind of confusion which makes men so lovable and so frightening (wanting to believe what they read, but at the same time fighting every idea). More than anything else, the thing that really halts our progress is the image which emerges from these writings of Woman as a special creature, a creature of uncommon prescience, of understanding of such depth that man can only estimate it, of such vision that, by comparison, Man is little more than a Cub Scout, of masterful intrigue and diplomacy, and, above all, a creature who is a victim of almost total misunderstanding.

It's that last we balk at. Women are understood much better than they think. It's an old stunt, when you're trying to get away with something, to take on an aura of mystery. Kids do it all the time, but with only moderate success, because other kids see through the trick instantly. We know what women want: they want tenderness, warmth, kindness, and compassion. But they shouldn't take it by force.

"WHERE DID YOU GO?" "UP." "WHAT DID YOU DO?" "COME DOWN."

There's not a great deal of money in the job of running an elevator, but for those who are watching with pleasure the steady decline of the human race (there are puns all through this piece), the work can be very attractive. In no other line of business do you have a better opportunity to observe the disintegration of society or to make occasional contributions to its eventual collapse. For those who are seeking an ataraxic profession, and who are eager to get started, we offer the following ground instruction which is sufficient to enable the beginner to solo:

1. There is only one answer to the friendly question, "How're things going?" and that is "Up and down." This isn't even funny the first time you hear it, and it gets almost unendurable when repeated morning after morning. You will soon notice that those who work on the first four floors, rather than encounter this repartee, will begin using the stairs.

2. Never forget that you have claustrophobia on your side and you couldn't have a more reliable ally. This, together with the fact that nobody really trusts the mechanism of an elevator, opens up a fascinating world for an operator with imagination. A simple exercise consists of closing the doors on a crowded car and pulling the plunger *just short* of what's necessary to start the elevator moving. Convinced the car is stuck, two or three of the most claustrophobic will wilt immediately.

3. Smile encouragingly at a hurrying passenger. Invariably he'll interpret the smile to mean you'll wait for him. Let him almost reach the gate before closing it.

4. Get the passengers braced for the ascent, then without warning drop to the basement. Several will be thrown off balance so badly they'll get off there and go home.

5. Level off between floors and fight with the controls. This is especially effective during the five o'clock rush period when man's resistance is at its lowest ebb.

6. Handling the inside extension gate is an art in itself and should be given separate study and practice. Actually, it presents the operator with some of his greatest opportunities for self-expression, and true virtuosity in this field is likely to be a lasting source of satisfaction and pleasure. Let a passenger permit a package to protrude across the track for one instant and an alert operator can atomize it. We once saw an operator remove a watch from a man's vest pocket with

the extension gate, but the operator later told us it was the first time he'd been able to get the watch. Twice before, he said, he had torn the vest.

7. You have to stop at the street floor and the top floor, but you can use your own judgment about responding to signals in between. Some operators, as a rule of thumb, pass the passenger three times before stopping; others wait until the passenger leans on the buzzer and holds it down. The decision is for the operator.

YOU CAN'T TRAVEL
WITHOUT CREDENTIALS

Today we are going to tell one of the most amazing and—to us—wonderful stories ever to come out of Washington. Our source affirms the story is true in every detail.

A citizen of West Germany, who was residing temporarily in the United States, died recently, and his relatives in this country decided to return the remains to Europe where they would be properly interred in his native soil. Inquiry was promptly made at the Department of Commerce. Was a freight manifest all that was necessary for a return of the body to the Reich? Reluctantly, the Commerce people said no. An export license was also required.

The relatives were grateful but confused and the Commerce people were polite but firm. A form was provided, and a Commerce official explained that in addition to other general information it would be necessary to state the general classification of the shipment.

"What should this classification be?" one of the relatives asked.

The Commerce official acknowledged that he didn't know but agreed to study the problem and promised an answer within the hour. Sixty minutes later, the U.S. Government was ready.

It could be done very simply, the Commerce official explained. An application must be made for an Export License to cover a—he paused and coughed lightly—Gift Shipment.

If the relatives were shocked, they concealed it nicely. They asked if anything else would be necessary.

The Commerce Department official said that, as a matter of fact, there was something else. This particular Export License could be issued only under a Schedule B Category, which in turn required a listing of the particular classification of the Gift Shipment. The Commerce man said he had already determined the only possible Schedule B Category for the case.

The apparent hesitation of the official to name this classification caused the relatives to brace themselves. After commenting on what a great help the Commerce Department had been to persons unaccustomed to such matters, one of the relatives inquired as to the allowable Schedule B Category.

The Commerce man fumbled nervously with his papers. "Under Schedule B," he said, "just insert 'Animal Products —unprocessed.'"

There was a brief pause, and again the relatives expressed their gratitude. As they turned away, the Commerce man said they knew, of course, about the Import License.

"Import License?" one of the relatives asked.

The Commerce man nodded. That would be a little more complicated, he explained, since it had to be gotten from the Aussenhandelskontor of the German Foreign Trade Office in Frankfurt.

"It may take a little time," he warned.

MAY WE SEE YOU A MOMENT, OUTSIDE?

There was a time, not too long ago it seems, when all we needed for a big evening was to come from the movies where we had seen Thomas Meighan push Doris Kenyon around, and set the knobs of our Atwater Kent to bring in Johnny Hamp's Kentucky Serenaders. Tiring of that, we'd wind up the phonograph and put on the Coon-Sanders recording of "Collegiate." Waring's Pennsylvanians had a tip-top recording of that too, but with the slats all the way open we seemed to detect a slight difference and it was in favor of Coon-Sanders.

But things are changed now. The last two movies we saw were not only turkeys, they were real barnyard champions, and about the time we get interested in a television drama a man comes on and starts to shave a peach. That's all we need to start us reaching for the light switch and groping for the stair railing. Like a lot of other people, we suspect, we have had to search out more rewarding pleasures, and we don't mind sharing our findings with others. All of the diversions listed here are simple, inexpensive, and can be fitted anywhere into the life of the individual. All are for adults and up.

1. A lot of fun can be had around the office, if you take the trouble to find it.

(a) Telephone your secretary that you will be in late, then arrange to get to the office five minutes early. You couldn't start the day out better.

(b) Tell your subordinates to "stand by" for some emergency night work, and rush out to an important conference. Return about 7:20 with an unsteady gait, and announce, rather thickly, that the crisis is over and no one need stick around any longer.

2. There's good, wholesome fun on the highway too if you are resourceful and imaginative.

(a) Come out of a side road fast and put on the brakes just before going on the highway. Synchronized properly with highway traffic, this can be immensely rewarding for one crowded second. Be prepared to turn around fast.

(b) Get a string of cars behind you on a narrow road and drop your speed down to about 19 miles per hour. Speed up when they try to pass. Flash your brake light continually at the car behind you, as this builds up anxiety in the driver. This maneuver is good anytime, but it is especially rewarding on Sunday afternoon.

3. In making a speech, give the audience about thirty minutes of dull oratory, and then say, "And in con-

clusion. . . ." Observe how long it takes the brightening look to give way to glazed eyes when you warm up again and talk for thirty minutes more.

4. Stand in the door of a streetcar or bus and argue with the driver over the route. Notice how eagerly he glances at the green light. As soon as the light turns red, step off and say you must have the wrong car. You'll get a tremendous lift from this, especially around 8:55 A.M.

5. Stop by the box office of a theater where a hit is playing. If it's a real hit, the ticket seller will be talking on the telephone, cradling the instrument on his shoulder. Cough several times, and then start tapping the glass counter methodically with a coin. When he puts the telephone down to come to the window, ask him which way is Eighth Avenue. Remember, bad language can be reported to the license commissioner.

Finally, a word of caution. We advise against repeating any of these pleasant exercises. Not only is it poor sportsmanship, it's also imprudent.

NO HANDS

A fellow we know, who travels around a lot, has always been curious about those terse, whispered conversations in which airline stewardesses engage when they pass each other in the aisles or meet at the coffee bar in the back of the plane. Much of this curiosity was dispelled recently, he told us, when a meeting took place right at his elbow and one stewardess murmured to the other: "Watch yourself if you have to take anything up front. They've got the automatic pilot on."

THE FLOWERS THAT BLOOM IN THE SPRING, HA! HA!

A few days ago the seed catalogue arrived, our only remaining link with rural living, and with no more waste motion than a fourth-grader shows in responding to the recess bell, we pushed aside the papers on our desk and plunged into the tomato section. But instantly something stirred in the back of our brain, and, like a cat recognizing that catastrophe lies one step forward in the darkness, we closed the catalogue firmly and dropped it in the wastebasket. It took only a minute to retrieve from a drawer four letters—written in agony three years ago while we were living on a farm in Pennsylvania—and we are going to publish them here as a public service. If it causes just one exurbanite to pause and think, our confession will have been worthwhile.

March 12

Mr. Lurty Ellis
R.F.D. 3
Perkasie, Pa.
Dear Mr. Ellis:

The seed catalogue arrived today and it is with a great deal of pleasure that I advise you that I intend to have a garden myself this year. This means that I will not be buying vegetables from you this summer and you may resume feeding them to your hogs—a course of action which, if agreeable to the hogs, should never have been disturbed.

Looking back over last summer, I can thank you for jading my appetite when nothing else would. What upset me most was not the fact that your vegetables looked like rejects from the commissary of a Nazi concentration camp, but that, unarmed, you could make me pay for them. I'll never forget paying you sixty cents for six small ears of corn, and to be perfectly frank I've seen better looking corn wash ashore from a garbage scow.

Well, that's all behind us now. I'm ordering my seeds today. Give my best regards to Mrs. Ellis and my deepest sympathy to the hogs.

Yours truly,
Caskie Stinnett

April 30

Mr. Lurty Ellis
R.F.D. 3
Perkasie, Pa.
Dear Mr. Ellis:

This last unseasonable frost nipped my Early All-Green Long-Tipped Asparagus, and, consequently, I'd like to order several bunches of asparagus from you. Please bring these over Saturday morning. I think I also lost my Mammoth Extra-Early Peas and I would like for you to include some peas in the order. My other vegetables are coming along nicely and after this I'll be eating my own produce. Sometime when you are passing this way take a look at my Hybrid White Sweet Corn. I'll be glad to get you something to stand on.

> Yours truly,
> Caskie Stinnett

June 16

Mr. Lurty Ellis
R.F.D. 3
Perkasie, Pa.
Dear Mr. Ellis:

I can't understand how your vegetables, which have always been only one jump ahead of compost, have survived the past four weeks of drought. Please let me have some beets, lima beans, lettuce, a few cucumbers, and some Swiss chard.

I'm watering my corn every night and it looks fine. When the ears fill out I'd like to show you one. You will be amazed to find that ears of corn often exceed three inches in length.

> Yours truly,
> Caskie Stinnett

July 12

Mr. Lurty Ellis
R.F.D. 3
Perkasie, Pa.
Mr. Ellis:

Please give my son 6 ears of corn. He has the ninety cents.

> Caskie Stinnett

THE PRICE OF PEACE
IS ON THE SCALES

Just outside of our office a new ticker has been chatter-
ing away the past few weeks with gloomy news from the
Middle East, Europe, and the Caribbean. Only today, on a
return trip from the water cooler, we noted that another
nation had frustrated U.N. plans, and that matters in the
Caribbean were taking a turn for the worse. But so far as we
are concerned, the news ticker is lagging far behind a more
sensitive and more reliable instrument for measuring the
world's illness, and if you want the news ahead of the news
our advice to you is to keep your eye on your local market
proprietor, whose insolence, like the mothball fleet, has only
been awaiting bad news for reactivation.

What brings this up is an experience we had with the
proprietor of our market, a man who is known in the neighborhood as a sort of reverse Robin Hood. He takes from the
poor and gives to the rich, the rich in this case always being
the owner of the store. When we entered the market a few
days ago he was arguing with a woman customer, and it was
easy to see that the Middle East situation was so unsettled
that he didn't know whether to be polite or not. With
Russia's threat to send volunteers to Egypt ringing in his ears,
he had come in early that morning to give his grocery clerk—
an obvious 4-F unless the Army has eliminated all intelligence
standards—an hour's rehearsal in sneaking coffee and sugar
from under the counter and into shopping bags, and the effect
of this had been to bring back to him the radiant war years
when a stern glance was enough to make a customer pull out
a handkerchief and wipe his fingerprints off the showcase.

"I know there's a lot of bone in the pork roast," he said to
the woman, "but the news is so contradictory right now that
I hardly know what to do. Yesterday, when the Hungarian
revolt looked bad for the Russians, I had to go back giving
full weight on all meat orders."

"Clopton's Market is not only cutting out the bone today
but they are also trimming off the fat," the woman said.

"Clopton's an alarmist," the man said. "He sees peace in every headline. Kindly hold your bundles in your arms, the counter is no checkroom."

We had pulled a grape from a bunch and were polishing it on our sleeve when the manager turned to us. His eye went to the grape.

"Things in Suez look all right to you, huh?" he said. It wasn't a question.

"Well, no," we said, "but the radio said this morning that the U.N. was going—"

"Don't mention U.N. to me," he said, holding up a hand. "Last week they put out a report that had me resuming deliveries for two days. I was humiliated."

We nodded in sympathy. It's easy to see how good news from the U.N. could mislead a man into becoming the laughing stock of the entire grocery, meat, and delicatessen field. "Isn't there some way that you can protect yourself from being pleasant if you don't have to?" we asked. "Have you tried—"

"I've tried everything," he said. "First, all editions of the newspapers. Then I put a radio in. Next week I'm having a news wire installed. That will make it possible for me to raise prices several times a day if circumstances warrant. But it all worries me."

"Why?" we asked.

"Well, my customers are going to have to pay for all this. I hate to think about it."

We put the grape back and started for the door. You can't steal a grape from a guy with a heart like that.

IT MAY COST A LITTLE MORE

We've contended for a long time that this mass-assembly mania can be carried too far, and now that it has happened we can't find the impulse to exult. It may be a little hard to grasp at first, but under our mass-assembly system one thing now often costs more than two. To illustrate, we'll relate what happened to us recently when we went to buy a slip cover for the front seat of the car.

"You want I should break a set?" the man in the auto-accessory department asked. It was as if we'd asked him to put the torch to his mother's cottage.

"The back seat has never been used," we explained, "because my wife prefers to give me instructions from the front seat." We laughed winsomely.

He didn't laugh.

"Half a set will run a good deal more than a full set," he said, noting with satisfaction that the smile had frozen on our lips. "We'll have to order it special, and that means special handling. They might even have to make it special, which would mean shutting down one machine for a whole day. A new car would be a lot cheaper—"

You would have thought that when we got to the garage later we would have been prepared for the installer, but we weren't.

"To install half a set," the garage man said, "will—"

"—Run a good deal more," we suggested.

"Exactly," he said, nodding to show his appreciation of our understanding. "Half a set requires special handling. Covers are put on by two men working as a team. Take out the back seat man, and there's nobody for the front man to talk to. He has to lower the window and talk to the other men in the shop. This slows everybody down. I'm glad you understand."

We took the slip cover home and put it on ourself. On the *car,* ourself. The only person we talked to was our wife and all we said was, "Hand me the pliers." It worked so well that we're thinking of installing half-sets for our friends. It sounds crazy—and it may take a while for the idea to catch on—but we plan on charging only half as much as for a full set.

WHERE'S THE STUDIO AUDIENCE?

We would like to exchange correspondence with someone who, like us, has had the measles, the whooping cough, or the mumps. There aren't many of us left, and it may be good if we could get together, like the Civil War Veterans, and swap experiences. In a world full of inhibition, depression, hypomania, neuroses, schizophrenia, conversion hysteria, and conflict between inner and outer personalities, it may even be a good influence. Anyway, if you would like to hear about our case of German measles in 1923—and there were some rather interesting details—just drop us a line.

Our attention was brought to this subject recently when we offered ourself for a physical examination, and instead of a kindly old physician with a blood pressure gauge and a stethoscope there were a doctor, a nurse, and a notebook. Although the nurse held the notebook and undoubtedly has the only official report of the proceedings, our recollection of it is as follows:

"First, we'll check him for Babinski," the doctor said, seizing one of our feet and dragging a nail across the bare sole. We almost rolled from the couch.

"Extreme Babinski," the doctor dictated, "with possible symptoms of Osgood Slater's Disease."

"What about Whitman's Disease?" the nurse asked, picking up a vicious-looking needle and purring softly.

"If he has it," the doctor replied with obvious satisfaction, "it would be so advanced an injection wouldn't help."

Rather petulantly, the nurse put the needle down. "How about Romberg?"

The doctor directed us to stand up, hold our feet together, close our eyes, and extend both arms. We did.

"Catch him, Doctor!" the nurse shouted.

They eased us back to the couch. "Not only Romberg," the doctor said, "but also locomotor ataxia."

"Bad?' the nurse inquired, her pad poised on our knee.

"So bad he probably whistles at crossings," the doctor replied.

The nurse jabbed us in the ribs. "Laugh it up," she said. "He doesn't pull a nifty like that often."

We were forcing a smile when the doctor approached with a pin. "This tests the integrity of the central nervous system," he explained. "Whenever you feel a pinprick, say 'Pin.' " He sank the pin into our thigh.

We said ouch.

"Unco-operative and refuses to take directions," the doctor dictated.

We were going to reply but the doctor effectively cut off any further comment by squeezing a minor nerve center between thumb and forefinger.

"You have Huntington's Teeth but I want you to take the test anyway," he said. "Put on the robe and walk down the hall until you come to Dental Lab."

We walked down the hall until we came to a taxi stand. The robe wasn't much but neither was the suit we left.

Later in the afternoon, we dropped in on our old family doctor for a checkup. When he put the thermometer under our tongue and got out his stethoscope, we felt perhaps he hadn't kept up with current medical progress, but when we left we felt like a million dollars.

OPERATION CHAMPAGNE

We witnessed a submarine launching in the newsreel the other day, and as usual there was a great deal of awkwardness in bringing bow and bottle together. In this case, the bottle missed the ship entirely, and the scene that followed took so much out of us, emotionally speaking, that we set about immediately probing the dark recesses of our subconscious to determine the source of the trauma. We were sweating out this attempt at total recall, when suddenly a realization leaped at us: we had never seen a launching where one of two things had not occurred. Either the bottle failed to break or else the christener's aim was so bad that it never hit the ship at all.

Our interest in this subject was born when we witnessed the christening, during wartime, of a light cruiser of the Indianapolis class. As usual, the champagne was apparently fabricated of stainless steel, and by the time the ship reached the water it had lost so much superstructure that it barely qualified for the Comet class. We heard later that it was put to use as a ferryboat, since both ends looked pretty much the same.

Although we didn't see it, we had a good account of a somewhat similar occurrence at another yard. Anticipating trouble, the Navy filed the glass in the bottle almost through. The filing turned out to be a complete waste of time, however, because in the tragic struggle which followed, the bow of the ship yielded first. It was the first sinking of an armed ship inside the three-mile limit to occur during the war.

The most respected person in ship-christening circles is the wife of a senator who, in the first year of the war, matched the Japs in ship sinkings, ton for ton. At one yard she hit a merchant ship a glancing blow which, while it didn't stave in the bow, did succeed in pieing the type on the name plate. The boat started down the ways as the S.S. GLEN COVE but it was the S.S. GVCL ENOE when it hit the water. On another occasion she took a one-arm swipe at a baby flattop and missed. From the ship's loudspeaker a voice said, "You never laid a glove on me." We don't know who said it, but it is the last thing he ever said because on the next try she connected. They're using it now as a breakwater just outside Charleston.

Of course the fear that constantly haunts Navy men is that the ship will move down the ways *before* the christener can get his licks in. We once saw this happen to a well-placed government man, and it was as unnerving an experience as we ever hope to encounter. The government man, naturally, was saying a few preliminary words, when the ship took off. We can't recall all that happened in the crowded, chaotic moments that followed, but when we looked back at the government man we saw that he had managed to get the cork out of the bottle. That's one way to handle a bad situation.

CERTAIN?

Our Washington man (whom we can't reward for these items because in meeting the government's new Sanitary

Code he had to relinquish all business connections) likes nothing better than to roam through the federal office buildings reading the signs on the walls. He found one in the Pentagon that he especially liked. It was on the wall of a major general and it said: "If you can keep your head when those around you are losing theirs—then maybe you don't understand the situation."

CODE

Every now and then we get overcome by sentiment about Hollywood and its quaint folkways, and when the mood is on us—as it is now—we can't resist sharing our feeling. Everyone has heard, of course, about the Hollywood actress who told her child that heart-warming old story about the Father Bear, the Mother Bear, and the Baby Bear by a former marriage. Well, a fellow just back from the Coast was telling us of something he overheard there recently which struck us as touching, almost as deftly, the soul of the community. A film director, exhausted from hours of tedious effort trying to make a beautiful young starlet understand the character she was playing, turned her over to an assistant with the admonition, "Wait until I've gone and then tell her she's got to come back tonight for r-e-h-e-a-r-s-a-l."

THERE'S NO BUSINESS LIKE THE FASHION SHOW BUSINESS

Things haven't been breaking too well for us lately. During the past month it's been our misfortune to attend three fashion shows and all we can say is that if circumstances ever get *within* our control again we'll never attend another one.

In the first place, is there any reason why a model should stand in such a way as to give the impression that her feet grew on backwards? And if she wants to look in the other direction, why doesn't she just turn around like anybody else instead of planting her feet in the rug and twisting her vertebra until the more nervous of us bite our lips and turn away? And has it been raining an awful lot lately? If not, what's the purpose of that rolled-up umbrella that's carried with everything including the housecoat?

What exasperates us most is the compulsion of the store to show every dress it has and in some cases, we suspect, to bring in a few from across the street. The first half hour or so finds us applauding the better-looking models and even tempted to whistle at the one in the short beach coat, but after that our interest wanes. At the end of the hour, our thought processes have slowed to a point where we are balancing on the edge of our chair with our mouth slightly agape. The second hour finds our eyes glazed over, and at the end of the third hour our hands are hanging lifelessly between our knees.

And the sound track! "With this periwinkle blue *peau de soie* cocktail dress, oh so cool and festive, comes an aurora borealis flounce . . ." the narrator says. Well, Narrator, we happen to know what flounce means, and we would like to do it now. Right out of here.

The one thing about the whole affair that interested us was the way the girls walked down the runway. We can remember when certain types of theaters featured that sort of entertainment and the recollection kept us occupied for some time. As a matter of fact, we were told later that when the curtain opened up, showing the runway, our eyes lit up like a pinball machine, but the radiance quickly died away.

LET'S GO OUTSIDE AGAIN

Man has figured out a lot of ways of making himself miserable, but the soundest idea he has hit on in a long while is to take a small child into a public restaurant. As nearly as we can figure it, this reduces everybody to the level of Pleistocene primates: the parents abandon hope of the child's developing normally; the waiter starts working out the proportion of chloral hydrate required for a junior-grade

Mickey Finn; the owner considers selling the restaurant and going to live with his son; and as for the other guests, three out of five will stop by the neighborhood library tomorrow morning and pick up *Malthus on Population*.

A child psychologist, whose name we will not reveal because of a genuine concern for his safety, now comes forward with the suggestion that the child should be given what's known as an object lesson. This involves taking a child to a restaurant and doing all the things the child does. We can understand how this would be gratifying to the child, but we shudder to think of the effect on the other customers. For example:

1. Knock the milk over, yourself. To beat the child to it you will have to strike with the speed of a cobra. Try to hit the glass in such a way that the milk flows across the table and into the lap of an adult. You will probably never achieve the casual, sure touch that the child displays, but you can do a good workmanlike job if you apply yourself spiritedly.

2. Kick the table so as to spill coffee into the saucers. A well-placed kick during the soup course can get the entire party moved to another table.

3. Twist around in your chair until, as nearly as possible, you have your back to the table. This permits you to see the coming and going of waiters, the seating of customers, and makes it possible to ignore the food completely.

4. Most of the food, of course, goes on the floor where it belongs, but a certain amount should be saved for the tablecloth. Spear the lamb chop violently and let the fork strike the plate a glancing blow. This *propels* the peas across the table, which is better theater than having them dribble over the sides of the plate.

5. As part of the squirming process, it is interesting to tip the chair over backwards. Though this contains some excellent possibilities for upsetting the entire restaurant, there is always the possibility of getting hurt, so it can be recommended only when other efforts to make the occasion memorable have failed.

6. It's good social custom to get down from the chair and

wander around other tables, staring at strangers and even inquiring what they are eating. This adds immeasurably to the
sociability of the meal.

These are the main points to remember in teaching the
child a lesson, but there's one other thing. Keep your eye on
the manager and be ready to leave as soon as you see him
make a furtive telephone call from the cashier's desk. If
there's a side door, take it.

TIES

We have always been fascinated, in a horror-stricken
sort of way, by those groups that are identifiable by their
neckties as being bound together by some academic loyalty
or regimental allegiance—those wearers of special colors or
plaids or designs which, in some mystic way, manage to en-
twine their sons and daughters by a common thread. In
England, where, we understand, the old school tie tradition
has attained its full growth, even corporate loyalties are sometimes expressed in this manner. Our attitude toward this sort
of thing is shared by Ted Patrick, a magazine editor, who not
long ago found himself involved—as good a word as any—in a
situation that to a less impious man would perhaps have
passed unnoticed. Patrick was in London, at the time, talking
with writers, when he had occasion one day to meet an author at Grosvenor House. Arriving a bit early, Patrick descended to the gentlemen's lounge to freshen up a bit when
his eye was caught by a glass case enclosing a handsome-look-
ing necktie. Upon examining the tie closely, Patrick noticed
that it contained a crest that he accurately concluded to be
the heraldic blazonry of Grosvenor House itself. Calling an
attendant, Patrick tapped the case and asked if the Grosvenor
House tie was for sale to the general public. The attendant
acknowledged that it was but felt constrained to add that
only guests of Grosvenor House would feel, well, comfortable
wearing the tie. "Do you have to show proof of registration,"
Patrick persisted, "or do you have to exhibit your room key?
Or is identification by the room clerk required? In other

words, what is to prevent a guest of Claridge's from coming in here to buy a Grosvenor House tie?"

The attendant's jaw sagged and his color fled as, for the first time, he contemplated the audacity of the possibility suddenly laid before him. "Now who, sir," he said in an awed whisper, "would do a thing like that?"

ALL TOGETHER, NOW

A fellow who ranges widely and who reports odd stories to us from all over, told us recently of a high school band concert he had attended recently on a courthouse green in a small town in upper New York state. Our friend was quite close to the band, and during the applause for one number he heard the trombonist ask, "What's the next number?"

The leader whispered, " 'The Washington Post March.' "

"No," gasped the trombonist, "I just finished playing that."

WILD WORLD NEWS

It's Spring.

The Manchester *Guardian,* a conservative and reliable British newspaper, showed concern that not a single British animal has so far gone out into space, and wondered if the nation's animals are not letting the country down. "Are British dogs growing soft?" the Guardian asked. Elsewhere the newspaper referred to a white rat, of no fixed address, that was reputed to be trying to make its way to Cape Canaveral, but we were left with the feeling that the *Guardian* was clutching at straws.

The United States House of Representatives voted $2500 for a gold medal for Poet Robert Frost after Congressman Clare Hoffman observed that the only good he could see in this was that the gold would undoubtedly remain in the country and thus be considered part of Mr. Kennedy's save-the-gold program. Sir Edmund Hillary, the conqueror of

Mt. Everest, drew a fine of 8000 Nepalese rupees for climbing Mt. Ama Dablam without advance authorization. Since charges are reckoned on the height of the peak, Sir Edmund considers himself lucky not to have suffered a lapse of memory on the Mt. Everest expedition. Pablo Picasso, seventy-nine, married a lady who was described by *The Spectator* as having "one eye on each side of her face." A new translation of the New Testament appeared in Great Britain and, in the first week, outsold *Lady Chatterley's Lover.*

Among the facilities now offered by a San Diego motel is a wedding chapel, which we see as a step in the right direction. Antarctic whales are reported to be adopting wartime convoy tactics to avoid slaughter by whalers. They scatter when attacked, a whaling ship captain said angrily, adding that this was one more argument for peace. In the House of Lords, an appeal was heard from a publisher's attorney who said his client performed a public service—"much like that of doctors and lawyers"—by issuing a prostitutes' guidebook. Elsewhere among professional people, a suit was filed by five Parisian prostitutes against the French national television system for something roughly equivalent to invasion of privacy. The defense cited the fact that the program, a documentary, was praised by critics, but the plaintiffs promptly struck back with the charge that the show was put on at eight-thirty in the evening, when children were still up, thus assuming the role of protectors of the morals of the youth of Paris.

In Memphis, Mrs. William H. Riley was granted a divorce after she testified her husband spent $900 on cablegrams to Khrushchev and Castro, at the same time allowing her only candles to light their home and insisting that their three children observe Jewish fast days, although the family is Protestant. Another yeasty event occurred in the South when federal agents, smashing a bootleg ring near Savannah, brought in under arrest a police chief and a deputy sheriff. One of five cars confiscated for allegedly transporting illegal whisky was a police car. In Scotland, a distillery workman turned the wrong tap and five thousand fifths of fine Scotch whisky drained into the River Bladnoch. Villagers, who regard an effort of this kind almost as a capital offense, estimated the loss totaled 153,906 shots. The most revealing thing in this to us (a consumer) is that a hasty slide-rule calculation turns up the disappointing fact that a Scottish shot is considerably less than an American ounce, or the near equivalent of a temperance drink.

The National Canned Pea Council opened National Pea Week with a drive to top last year's reported average of eleven peas a day for every man, woman, and child in the United States. The new goal was not reported.

SPRING TRIP

We have the standard admiration for little old lady stories, especially when they are as true as the one that we are about to relate. The maiden aunt of a friend of ours, who lives in a Midwestern city, has a habit of spending a week in New York each spring, seeing the shows, buying some clothes, and living it up in a lady-like sort of way. Having grown fond of a small West Side hotel, she always establishes herself there, and her first act of business, after her bags have been set down, is to step out into the hallway and check on the location of the fire exits. On her most recent visit she was a little disconcerted to notice that there had been some remodeling of the hotel, and when she went to make her annual checkup, there was no fire exit visible from her door. Resolutely she marched to the end of the hall and opened the last door on her left. Instantly, she found herself facing an elderly gentleman seated in a bathtub. "Pardon me," the lady said, backing out hurriedly. "I'm looking for the fire escape." She had scarcely gotten halfway back to her door when the man, dripping wet but with a towel draped around him, caught up with her. "Where's the fire?" he asked anxiously.

3

The Four Seasons

SUMMER

SEASONAL NOTES: Things looked bad this week, so bad, in fact, that the San Francisco papers reported that Lucius Beebe's bomb shelter was being stocked with champagne and caviar against the day of reckoning. In Washington the gravity of our time was emphasized when Dr. Bentley Glass, a scientist, submitted a report to the Government which later refused him permission to re-examine it on the ground that he wasn't cleared for access to such top-secret material. The Prix Jules, awarded in Paris for the worst book of the year, went to the wife of Bernard Buffet, the artist, for her novel, *L'Amour Quotidien* (*Daily Love*), the title of which alone suggests enormous reprint possibilities in this country. Elsewhere in the world of literature, the Fake Book Jackets Company, of 60 East 42nd Street, New York, announced as an addition to its line, *How to Lose Gracefully at Russian Roulette*. The police offensive against nudity on the beach of St. Tropez reached the point where cops were patrolling the area in helicopters, the first time, undoubtedly, that French police were actually up in the air over public nakedness. French delegates to the Moscow trade fair, understandably alert to the possibilities of their hotel room being bugged, cut through a maze of multicolored wires they found hidden under the carpet. The floor was thick but not so thick that it deadened the sound of the chandelier crashing in the room beneath them. Subversion suffered another setback when a post-mortem performed on a dead seal at the Seattle Zoo revealed three hundred twenty-one pennies, twelve nickels, eight dimes, and one German pfennig in its stomach. It was officially announced that the pfennig was minted in *West* Germany, much to the relief of everyone. A hopeful pigeon, whose nest sits on the ledge of a Tulsa newspaper building —just outside of the photo lab—is at this moment trying to hatch two eggs and a flash bulb. There's not a delegate at the U.N. who doesn't know how she feels.

SEASONAL NOTES: The London *Sunday Times* has got to stop it. A few weeks ago the paper published an item that contained nothing more than an announcement of the award of "the Royal Victorian Medal to a yeoman bedgoer." We feel that's not the full story. The shoe was on the other foot, so to speak, in Rome, where a manufacturer issued a very long statement explaining why, in the future, he intended to make ladies' shoes that would fit either foot. It was news to us, and we suspect to the spirit of D. H. Lawrence, to learn that the London *Sunday Pictorial* is carrying a story called "Lady Chatterley's Daughter," a literary development that brings "Son of Hamlet" a little closer to reality. *France Soir,* of Paris, gravely announced last week that "the highest form of animal life is the giraffe," and in Chattanooga, Tennessee, twenty-six college boys announced with pride that they had crowded at one time into a compact car—a revelation that certainly adds some support to *France Soir's* contention. The Ocean City (Maryland) Bus Line found it necessary to post a sign saying, "Anyone carrying more than three watermelons will be charged for space." After the University of North Dakota administration building was condemned as "unsafe for human occupancy," it became the office of the school's president. In an economy move J. Paul Getty, one of the world's richest men, passed a test for a British driver's license, while in a public-spirited mood Miss Connie Jeffries, thirty-six, stepped onto a fire escape of the Hotel Cavalier, on New York's Third Avenue, and, totally nude, sang a song. Mr. Getty drives a Cadillac and Miss Jeffries sang "Yellow Bird." A shepherd in the Abruzzi Mountains, of Italy, bit a marauding bear on the nose, thus saving his flock, while in Houston, Texas, four men who had placed an overseas call to Brigitte Bardot showed an amazing lack of courage when the French film actress came to the phone. They couldn't think of a thing to say, but we have no assurance that the shepherd would have, either. Thus, other things than conscience make cowards of us all.

FURTHER NOTES: In an effort to find out how much fakery exists among art lovers, a Nice dealer placed an unsigned Modigliani, worth $10,000, on sale for $24. No one offered to buy it. In Texas H. L. Hunt, often described as one of the richest men in the world, showed uneasiness at proposals to print United States paper currency in different colors. "People are thoroughly accustomed to handling money the way it is," Mr. Hunt said, possibly overlooking the fact that some are more accustomed to it than others. In upstate New York a grocer, thinking to have a lark, put "instant water" on sale and did surprisingly good business with it, while in downtown New York City detectives of the Narcotics Bureau brought in a man who had been caught smoking mentholated —but unfiltered—marijuana. A talking myna bird was removed from public display at the Baltimore Zoo after someone taught it to say two words which did no credit to the teacher, the zoo, or the myna bird. In Manchester, England, workmen painted an artificial window on a slum property to brighten things up for a visit later by Queen Elizabeth II. We admire this spirit of social reform, and our only regret is that the occupants of the dwelling cannot get a glimpse of their monarch through their new *trompe-l'oeil* window.

AUTUMN

SEASONAL NOTES: Municipal pigeon catchers in Verona, Italy, mixed sleeping drugs with bird food to help rid the city of a surplus pigeon population. The drugged birds are being sent to other Italian towns where, it is presumed, those pigeons that are hooked will be given help in kicking. Scientists at Eastern Washington College puts rats in situations that frustrated them and then offered them a choice of water or an alcoholic solution. All of the rats developed a definite preference for the alcoholic solution, some requesting a twist of lemon peel. The admirable discretion of the French was the high point of the Mt. Blanc cable disaster, where police refused to disclose the names of the eighty-one persons rescued from the stranded cable cars. "You never know who travels with whom," a policeman said, "and in France we try to be as discreet about these things as we can." In St. Petersburg, Florida, where the telephone company recently converted its dial system, the unlisted number of Dr. Bradley Waldron was changed. When Dr. Waldron telephoned information to ask his new number, they refused to tell him. Martinsville, Virginia, proclaimed itself the "Sweatshirt Capital of the World," and, as yet, no city has sought to challenge this distinction. The schools of Little Rock, Arkansas, were further integrated but the big news out of that city was the arrest of a woman for walking down the street nude on a day when the temperature reached ninety-six degrees. City officials said they were sorry the newspapers did not give this event the same photographic coverage they gave the school riots, a sentiment echoed by many readers. *Time* magazine, in a report from Laos, said that King Savang Vatthana "thought he knew just how to start getting the warring factions on better terms: have them all up to the royal capital of Luangprabang late this month for the cremation of his father, old King Sisavang Vong, who has been preserved in formaldehyde since 1959." It sounds like a hell of a blast, and we're sorry our social calendar is so crowded.

INFLATIONARY NOTE

A fellow we know, who commutes from Evanston to Chicago, told us of a panhandler he often encounters on Michigan Avenue. A few days ago, he said, he had dropped a coin in the man's cup when he noticed another cup in the other hand, and curious, he paused to ask what that was for. "Business has been so good lately," the panhandler replied, "that I've had to open up a branch office."

WONDERS OF NATURE

There's no city like Philadelphia, you can bet your life on that. On a beautiful autumn day recently, one of those crisp, bright ones when there wasn't a cloud in the sky, a fellow we know found himself walking along Chestnut Street behind two middle-aged ladies who were discussing the weather. One had just commented on what a grand day it was, and the other nodded. "Wouldn't you just love to hang out a wash on a day like this?" she asked wistfully.

EDUCATIONAL NOTE

From Minneapolis, where the Pratt School is located, comes a notification to the effect that the local PTA group there is hard at work on the annual Pratt Fall Festival.

WINTER

DECK THE HALLS

We've just come from a meeting where we heard two men, one a former member of the Atomic Energy Commission and the other the director of one of our atomic laboratories, talk about nuclear energy, and more than ever we are inclined to agree with Sam Goldwyn when he said, "They shouldn't fool around with that stuff—it's dynamite." We learned that Russian planes now known to exist can bring a bomb to New York with such speed that a maximum warning of only twenty minutes would be possible, that it would take exactly seven days to evacuate New York City, and that within twenty seconds after one bomb fell the entire city would be a cinder. On the basis of this deadly schedule, before a single Manhattan school could be emptied, the building would become carbon isotopes.

This is a gloomy note on which to start an item about Christmas, the birthday of the Man called the Prince of Peace, but if you will stick with us we promise some cheer, too. A few weeks ago we heard another famous nuclear physicist (don't ask us what circle we've been moving in lately; we like to think it's just a case of water seeking its level) say, "And even those who live here (the house of science) live elsewhere also, live in houses where the rooms are not labeled atomic theory or genetics or the internal combustion of the stars, but quite different names like power and production and evil and beauty and history and children and the Word of God."

In Independence Square now, just beneath our window, a squirrel is energetically snatching peanuts from a gentleman sitting on a bench, and is scurrying up a tree with them. The cold weather has him frightened—not all summer or fall has he rushed around like this—and he isn't heartened any by the knowledge that his world (Independence Square), like ours, has shrunk. There are taxicabs and trucks now that don't give twenty minutes, or even twenty seconds, warning, but to evacuate the Square is unthinkable. Right now he isn't nearly as worried over radioactive fall-out as he is over the imminence of snow, which is about as damaging a fall-out as a squirrel can think of since it covers the nuts he has spotted throughout the Square and reduces the number of visitors bringing in fresh supplies. Things look tough.

Well, as we write this, the plane hasn't approached New York, the snow hasn't yet blanketed the Square, and the scientists still figure a place in the scheme of things for beauty, children and the Word of God. It's tenuous but it's there. Merry Christmas, *everybody*. Peace on earth, good will toward men.

WHEN OUT ON THE ROOF THERE AROSE SUCH A CLATTER . . .

Most writers, we've noticed, deal lyrically with spring, summer, and autumn, their hearts and typewriters beating out a sort of *allegretto grazioso* rhythm that provokes fine seasonal visions: children playing in schoolyards under the yellowing maples of autumn; brooks gurgling through green meadows after the first thaws of spring; voices echoing across a lake on a drowsy, summer afternoon. But who speaks for winter? Here the rhythm slows down to a leisurely murmur, or fades away entirely. It's not easy to be lyrical about handkerchiefs, overshoes, and inhalators.

Winter is a negative project and it follows a negative pattern, and ours is not the voice to speak up in its behalf. But we do speak up for Christmas—the Big Attraction without which winter could hardly remain in business—because we have a deep feeling that this grand sentimental lark, coming as it does at the end of a tough year (aren't they all?) is fine therapy for young and old alike. Moreover, it has the odd quality of being all things to all people, a further enhancement of its value now that the atom has backed us into a corner. Here is something that we can all grab hold of with vast satisfaction: the devout, the errant, the wistful, and the National Retail Credit Council. The churchman, on his way to midnight services, encounters one of his brethren making uneven progress home from the office party, a paper cup crumpled in his hand, and a crimson smear testifying to the partial collapse of a file clerk's year-long resistance. They pass, for perhaps the only time of the year, in mutual forbearance. A strange sort of reason seems to prevail.

We have spent the last few Christmases in a small village in Maine, and they have convinced us that the people outside of

New England don't know how to get their money's worth out
of Christmas. (This surprised us, too, because we had felt
that Christmas in Virginia, which we recalled from our child-
hood, had been all that you could expect.) Christmas and
New England go together; the natural conservationist there
has resisted efforts to hang too much tinsel or to make it
spurious. The air is crisp and cold, snow falls according to
some high-level prearrangement, church bells ring, children
sing, blazing logs light up hearths, and long-forgotten uncles
show up bearing armfuls of gifts. Metro-Goldwyn-Mayer
couldn't do it any better. But here, like everywhere else, the
season ends and what has been called the spirit of Christmas,
like the decorations, is taken down and stored away until
needed again. We aren't manic enough to want to live all
year in the buoyant atmosphere of Christmas Week, and one
office party a year is about all that our nervous system is con-
ditioned to absorb. But that mutual forbearance appeals to
us tremendously. It could be the warm sun around which we
could revolve all year, cheering us to the point where—who
knows?—perhaps we may even write a lyrical piece about
winter.

DECK THE HALLS WITH
WREATHS OF FOLLY

For the last few weeks we've been keeping an eye
cocked on Independence Square, watching impatiently for
the first sign of snow. It's our belief that a snowfall is as
necessary a prelude to Christmas as the dimming of the house
lights is to the opening of a play. One year there was no
snow, and so far as we were concerned, no Christmas. We
were on a freight ship, working a course through the Caribbean, and although that Christmas Eve was one of the most
beautiful nights in our memory—an oversized tropical moon
lighting the night in a ridiculous way—it could as easily have
been Guy Fawkes' Day as Christmas. We sat on a hatch cover,
listening to carols coming from the radio shack, then gave up
in disgust and wandered back to the crew's quarters in the

forecastle, where a case of Scotch was being rudely decanted. That much, *at least,* bore the authentic stamp of Christmas.

No, to be a success at all, Christmas must be unmistakably Christmas, and we don't know how it could get off to a better start than with a nice, gentle snowfall in Independence Square. There's something about the spectacle of snowflakes swirling around the gas lights and clock tower, and settling against the ancient brick buildings, that brings a classical Dickensian image to mind and scatters all suspicion that the National Retail Credit Association is the Hidden Persuader behind the event. If we seem over-anxious for the snow to arrive on schedule (or you might say even a little feverish about it) it's due to a deep-lodged fear that the time may not be far off when anything that falls from heaven will contain, not the quality of mercy, but Strontium 90, and it's our contention that a radioactive snowflake is no snowflake at all.

We've had a hand, in our time, in rolling many a snow man, and we'd like to pass on some of our technique to our children and grandchildren but not if they've got to be told to stand back until after the snow man is decontaminated or until a test is run to determine how much of a clatter the snow man sets off in a Geiger counter. Between Admiral Strauss and Scrooge, we must say that Scrooge remains our favorite Christmas character, although there are undeniably some similarities between the two.

And if there is one other thing that could make our Christmas complete this year and restore in us a feeling of good will it would be for Sputnik II to come to earth with a gentle bump in some small New England village and for Laika, the little Russian husky, to get out, stretch, sniff the fresh air, and follow some nice lady home. A dog's place at Christmas is in front of a hearth, not in a sealed container moving at 18,000 miles per hour in outer space. The idea.

NO BUSINESS LIKE SNOW BUSINESS

We wrote a pleasant, forgettable little Christmas piece, in which we spoke wistfully about snow, and we were swamped by letters, both of which were critical. John D. Weaver, a well-known (and doubtless well-to-do) Hollywood writer, described this cheerfully as "The most vomitous of all Yule clichés. The original Christmas, if you would stop to reflect, was anything but white. It was very much like the one we had here, warm and sunny. But without smog." The other letter was from an advertising man (whose name we aren't going to use because we know what side of our bread the margarine is on) who passed on the story of a Minneapolis girl of his acquaintance who journeyed to Texas to spend Christmas with an elderly aunt. The girl spent most of the preholiday season gazing out the window and muttering about the implausibility of a Christmas without snow. Finally the aunt's patience gave way, and she snapped: "Honey, whatever made you think that Jesus Christ was born in a snowstorm?"

FOOTNOTE TO WALDEN

During the height of a blizzard, one of the Philadelphia radio stations went on the air with a list of events that faced cancellation unless the snowfall stopped. The announcement that we like best, though, follows verbatim: "The Back-to-Nature Club will hold its scheduled hike tomorrow provided the Market Street subway is operating."

4

The Human World

Trying to write something new about James Thurber is like trying to write something new about the Civil War—somewhere it's all been done before. But we once decided to call on the famous essayist, novelist, playwright, short-story writer, humorist, and author, if for no other reason than to meet him and to learn what he was up to. At the time of our visit, Thurber was vacationing at the Wake Robin Inn, at Lakeville, Connecticut, having just completed a piece on the Loch Ness monster, and we found him, without difficulty, sunning himself on the hotel porch. A tall, spare man with a shock of gray hair and a close-cropped mustache, he offered us a chair, and launched into an account of a work schedule that would have dismayed a Marine sergeant. "Harper's is publishing a new book of mine, called *Alarms and Diversions,* in November," he said. "Right now I'm working desperately to meet a deadline on a new book for spring publication. It's a book about Harold Ross, who used to be editor of *The New Yorker.* I started this a few years ago and did a fast draft of about twenty thousand words. I knew Ross and worked with him for twenty-five years, and this increases the difficulty of the piece because I have so many memories of him. He was such an unusual person that even in a book I can only give glimpses of him. It's heartbreaking to have to throw out so much material. The major problem of writing about Ross is, as Wolcott Gibbs once said, 'If you get him right, nobody will believe him.' He was the most remarkable man I have ever known."

We asked Thurber if he would do any drawings for the book, and he shook his head. "I haven't drawn for five years," he said, "because I can now see nothing but light. The last drawing I did for publication was in 1951—six years ago. It was a self-portrait for a *Time* cover story. I started to go blind in 1940, and the drawing gradually became harder and harder. Someone in England sent me some dead black paper and a yellow, luminous crayon that glowed, and for a while I drew that way. Then I had to give it up entirely. The book may contain some of my drawings, but they will be ones I did while Ross was alive and which I gave to him. I used to do drawings satirizing the way the art department of *The New Yorker* was run, and they became a joke among the staff. Ross would take them around the office and ask, 'Is that funny?' You could never tell from his attitude whether he thought they were or were not." Thurber edged his chair slightly out of the sun. "I have a fine idea for a piece I'm going to write for a magazine," he said. "I think the editors will like it. The title is 'Such a Phrase As Drifts Through Dreams.' The idea came to me at a cocktail party in Bermuda, and it concerns the strange ways that people change words and phrases. A girl told me she didn't like professors because they had a habit of looking down each other's noses at people. Another girl told me that her apartment had been broken into so many times that she finally had to have it burglarized. For a while I thought this was a conspiracy to drive me insane. Now I intend to broaden the subject to include some mistakes caught in proofs, as well as some famous sayings and poems whose meaning is changed by one or two letters. 'In

Flanders Field the puppies growl,' is an example. My wife is a wonderful editor and is fine with proofs, and she has caught many of these slips. Ross was a great admirer of her's and once wrote a note thanking her for something she had done, and added a postscript: 'Your husband's opinion about any practical matter has no value whatever.' "

About two years' work went into the Loch Ness monster piece, Thurber told us, and much of this time was spent working with clippings covering a period of twenty-three years. "No British journalist had ever done a round-up story on the monster," he went on. "I did the piece straight. My wife and I went over on a boat and the second day at sea I started getting calls from the wire services wanting to know if I was going to be jolly funny about it. Gosh no. A London *Daily Express* man got on the boat at Plymouth and rode to France to talk to us about the Loch Ness monster."

We inquired if the loss of his sight had cut seriously into the quantity of his writing, and he shook his head. "I've written fourteen books since I went blind," he said. "Sometimes I think I can get more done this way. One day I went to lunch with Ross and he said, 'I can never sit down at a table without reading the label on this goddam Worcestershire sauce bottle.' I said, 'The trouble with you, Harold, is that you're not blind.' "

(*Author's Note:* The death, on November 2, 1961, of James Thurber was a loss that is still difficult to measure. We grieved at the departure of a personal friend, but his absence from the ranks of contemporary writers still shocks and dismays. His place has not been filled and we see no sign that it soon will be. But wherever there is human folly, corruption, or sham, there is also likely to be an anguished cry out of limbo, a signal that the wrath of the Thurber conscience is beginning to stir. This kindly but caustic man possessed a vital inner life that was remarkable to observe, even when the loss of sight caused him to sit still while the world wheeled by his window. He was curious, imaginative, artful, and irreplaceable.)

JOE McCARTHY

Joe McCarthy, a writer with a fine prose style, was sent to Ireland to do a story for a magazine. Although both of his parents came from Ireland, McCarthy had never been there and this curious fact formed the basis of his story. A few days ago we encountered McCarthy and inquired if anything had occurred to him in the old country that he had not included in the article, and he replied that, as a matter of fact, something had happened and he would like to tell us about it. He steered us gently into a bar, demanded a Bloody Mary for himself, and then leaned toward us across the table in a manner of a man beginning a story.

"Bear with me on a bit of background," he said. "A few years ago John McNulty, an Irishman who had never been to Ireland, did somewhat the same sort of thing for *The New Yorker.* I think his piece was called "Back Where I Had Never Been." Well, McNulty's story told of going to Kerry and visiting a famous Irish storyteller in a town called Waterville. He stayed at a hotel called the Butler Arms, and he asked a redheaded barmaid at the hotel where he could find a real Irish storyteller. She said she didn't know, but she directed him to a scholar and a student of Irish law named Taj Murphy. This fellow knew what McNulty was looking for, and he took him to a small village where there was a storyteller, and McNulty said he sat in front of a peat fire and listened to this beautiful story which was told with the color and cadence of a song. It was great.

"Three days after the piece came out in *The New Yorker,* I met McNulty on the street and I told him I had enjoyed the article, particularly the part about the old story-spinner. 'Want to know something confidential?' McNulty asked me. I said yes. 'He was the damnedest old bore I ever met in my life,' McNulty said. 'I couldn't use his story, so when I got back I went to the public library and got a really *good* story out of a book of Irish folk tales.' "

McCarthy held up his hand to keep us from interrupting.

"Now," he continued, "the scene shifts. It's 1962 and I'm in Waterville. I'm staying at the Butler Arms Hotel, and I go down to the bar and there is this redheaded barmaid there. I asked if she could make a Martini and she said that she could. And she did, a very good one I might add. Very casually, I said, 'Do you remember John McNulty, an American writer who was here a few years ago?' She said, 'I certainly do because he mentioned me in the article he wrote. How is he?' I said I was very sorry to have to tell her that Mr. McNulty had passed away. She expressed regret, and said that McNulty had asked her for an Irish storyteller and that she had passed him on to Taj Murphy who, in turn, took him to the village of Bally Skellegs to see a storyteller.

"I told her what McNulty had told me about the old man being a terrible bore, and she said she didn't wonder. 'Didn't Mr. McNulty tell you that the old man only spoke Gaelic and that he didn't understand a word he was saying?' I said McNulty hadn't mentioned that fact. 'It's true,' she said. 'Taj Murphy had to translate for him and I guess he did spend a very boring hour. Well, in any case Mr. McNulty is dead, Taj Murphy is dead, but the storyteller is still alive.' "

NEW AUTHORESS

We keep our eye firmly fixed on the literary horizon and we encourage you to look here for portents. Just a few days ago, for example, we had lunch with an authoress named Olivia de Havilland, and if her name sounds familiar to you it is possibly because she does a little acting as a side line. Miss de Havilland's first book—but not her last, we gathered quickly—was published recently by Random House under the title *Every Frenchman Has One,* and is a sprightly volume describing the basic problems involved in transplanting one's life from one country to another, in this case from America to France, following her marriage to a French journalist. An animated, talkative young woman with a nimble wit, Miss de Havilland told us she was vastly excited at discovering herself an authoress and that she planned to go right on writing.

"Do you know the first thing I ever wrote?" she asked us, and before we could shake our head she had started on the answer. "Years ago, I had a great romance with John Huston, the film director and writer. John's grandmother was a very remarkable old lady and we were both very fond of her. She died suddenly, and John asked me to prepare and deliver a eulogy for her funeral service. I had never done anything like this before, and I worked very hard, writing, in long-hand, what I thought should be said. I showed it to John with a great deal of uneasiness, and I was astounded when he handed it back to me and said, 'Say it just like that.' He didn't change a word."

However auspicious this beginning may have been, it was some time before Miss de Havilland got around to writing the current book. "I want to make it clear that I wrote this book," she said. "Every word in it is mine. I think Gerold Frank, who writes so many movie stars' biographies, was wounded at such a betrayal. The book is not about an actress but about a woman, an American woman adjusting to French life. I was first asked to write a book about Hollywood, but nothing funny ever happened to me there. My family laughed when I sat down at my Olivetti, but I kept at it. I gave the manuscript to my husband to read, and when he finished the first chapter he just said, '*Tres bien.*' Then he read the second chapter and said '*Bon.*' When he finished he said nothing, just picked up his newspaper. Isn't that exasperating? But I intend to get even. My play ends in a couple of weeks and my husband has already telephoned to entreat me to fly home to Paris immediately to arbitrate a dispute between the cook and the maid. Do you know what I'm going to do? I'm going by boat."

We asked Miss de Havilland if she preferred writing to acting, and she nodded affirmatively. "I'm a writer," she said brightly. "I'm just disguised as an actress. I would like to write fiction, but I don't know how to make the transition. The thought of fiction is sort of terrifying, but I love to read good fiction. I was in Switzerland in December a year ago, and I picked up a July issue of an American magazine and read 'The Light in the Piazza' by Elizabeth Spencer. I thought it one of the most wonderful stories I had ever read. Months later I was in Switzerland again, working on this book, incidentally, when I got a call from Culver City. It was a film producer asking if I would play in the motion-picture version of 'The Light in the Piazza.' I said yes and two months later I was in Florence, working in the film."

Whether writer or actress, Miss de Havilland is finding herself occupied with writers' problems. "I'm a fast writer," she said somewhat anxiously, "if my subconscious has done its work. By that I mean if things have been subconsciously organized. If not, I've struck a snag, and whatever I write comes with difficulty. But isn't this true with most writers?"

IN ONE ERA AND OUT THE OTHER

For the connoisseurs of the simply awful, those who are not satisfied with the dull and mediocre but who are looking for the pure distillate of inanity, we recommend the newspaper column of Miss Elsa Maxwell. Unfortunately the column has to be read to be believed, because we know of no other way that its quality can be conveyed. However, in the paragraphs that follow, we will try.

Miss Maxwell, as you already know, is a member of international café society, and though she travels around a lot, just like brandy in a snifter, she apparently never *gets* anywhere. It seems that Miss Maxwell can't escape from herself, and if she could she apparently doesn't think the ends justify the effort. In a very long column recently, one that revealed none of the writer's gifts except stamina, she told of a trip to Paris. Upon arrival at LeHavre, Miss Maxwell counted her luggage and told her readers that the three members of her party had thirty-three pieces of luggage "and I don't think even the Duchess of Windsor could beat that." If this in any way suggests some degree of self-satisfaction, just wait. In the next paragraph, Miss Maxwell shows that she has every reason to be pleased with herself. "The boat train reached Paris at noon," she wrote, "and I was photographed when I stepped

off the boat at LeHavre by French newspaper cameramen."
Miss Maxwell has a rather labyrinthine literary style that by
comparison makes Louella Parsons seem like Alfred Lord
Tennyson. "When we reached the Gare St. Lazare, another
one photographed and interviewed me. Arriving at the Ritz
(where I have stayed all my years abroad) was just a joy, everyone from Robert, the concierge, to the hall porter was smiling."

Miss Maxwell's visit to Paris lasted only twenty-four hours
and then she was off to Spain. "When we arrived in Seville,
we were met (I don't want to boast!) by the car and chauffeur
of Generalissimo Franco, who kindly sent it for me," she
wrote. And later she added: "Of course, the newspapers started
calling as soon as I had arrived, wanting interviews and photographs of your poor EM, who was pretty tired to be interviewed. One photographer took some lovely shots of me. . . ."

Generalissimo Franco offered Miss Maxwell his car again
the next day and before we could start speculating on this,
we were informed that this "unbelievably generous gesture"
was due to the fact that "I am a great friend of Spain." At
this point, Miss Maxwell herself becomes generous and ac-
knowledges that former President Eisenhower *also* did something or other to endear himself to Spain, a grouping that we
suspect General Eisenhower will greet with a somewhat mod-
ified rapture.

But if you think Miss Maxwell wears lightly her mantle of
international statesmanship, let us quote you another paragraph: "I had a sweet letter, too, from Tony Biddle saying
how sorry he was not to be in Madrid to welcome me when I
arrived. The Biddles are so nice, and I shall tell all my friends
in Madrid how charming His Excellency, our new American
Ambassador, is."

You can't get off to a better start than that, can you, Tony?

A TALK WITH JOHN STEINBECK

John Steinbeck, whose novel *Sweet Thursday* had
been made into a Rodgers and Hammerstein musical, agreed

to meet us recently in New Haven, where the show was trying out. We met him at the Schubert Theatre, where a rehearsal had just ended. Steinbeck was standing on the stage
when we approached him, surrounded by several actors,
production technicians, and Jo Mielziner, who designed the
scenery for *Pipe Dream,* the title of the musical.

"Jo," Steinbeck was saying, "those details look good."

"I think so, too," Mielziner replied. "I'm real pleased."

"There's going to be music this afternoon," said a man,
standing nearby.

"Wonderful," said Steinbeck.

A few moments later, Steinbeck came over to us and shook
hands warmly. "Let's get some lunch," he said. "The Ham-
mersteins are going to join us, if you don't mind. We all eat
across the street at Kaysey's. If it weren't for Kaysey's there
would be no theater in New Haven."

Seated in the restaurant, Steinbeck ordered a double Scotch
and soda, and turned to us. "This venture into the musical
theater is a new experience to me," he said. "It's fantastic,
the organization that is required. I dramatized *Of Mice and
Men,* and I've worked with movies, but this business of stag-
ing a musical is unbelievably complicated. I'm enjoying it
immensely, and I'm making a pretense of being necessary but
I'm not." We asked if the show were interfering with his
writing, and we were slightly startled when he replied negatively. "I write all the time," he said. "Writing is a sort of
nervous tic with me. I would go crazy if I didn't write. Much
of what I write, I throw away. In all of my books, with the
exception of *East of Eden,* what is published represents about
one-fifth of what I actually wrote. With *East of Eden* I threw
away a great deal more than four-fifths of the total manuscript. Right now I'm doing a number of short stories, and
a few weeks ago I completed four of them in one week. One
of the four I think is excellent. I have a story in my head
now that I've wanted to write for two years. I've thought
about it a lot, and I know it pretty well, but I've never hit
on an approach to it. It will come to me, and I'll know when
I'm ready for it. I suppose it will be a novel, although I've

never been sure exactly what a novel is. Something over thirty-five thousand words, I guess."

Steinbeck said that he had recently undergone a revolution in his writing and that nothing he was doing now would bear any resemblance to his past work. "I'm through with those characters," he said, pointing toward the theater to indicate the *Cannery Row* and *Sweet Thursday* characters that people *Pipe Dream,* "as well as all of my old props, and techniques, and styles. I may be making a mistake but, hell, they can't put you in jail for being wrong. I used to be too facile. All of my stories now are different, not only different from each other but different from anything I have done in the past. This is very exciting for me, and I enjoy writing now more than I ever did. I can't tell you how satisfying it is to start a new story with no thought of old styles or old approaches."

We brought Steinbeck around to the subject of a recent magazine piece on Paris. "This was one of a series I did over a year ago when I was living in Paris," he said. "I did twenty-five or twenty-six short pieces for the literary section of Figaro. The idea was ridiculous—an American writing in English for translation into French a series of articles about France. I wandered around, asked a lot of questions, and from my standpoint it was a rich experience. It must have been a good series for Figaro, too, because the mail response was fantastically high, and the French people are not letter writers." We asked Steinbeck if he had written anything since he had been in New Haven with the show. "Hell, I just got here last night," he replied. "But I'll probably start tomorrow. Or the next day."

MEANWHILE, BACK AT THE PALACE FLOPHOUSE . . .

Cannery Row, on the Monterey Peninsula of California, was only a few blocks long, but its inhabitants had a great grasp of human values. There was the Palace Flophouse, the home of Mack and the boys who were united by a common dislike of a steady job and a common fondness for a four-month-old whiskey labeled Old Tennessee but called Old Tennis Shoes by its devotees, while across the street was the marine laboratory run by Doc, who played Gregorian music with the blinds down and who loved sick puppies, children, and unhappy souls. It was sixteen years ago that John Steinbeck presented Mack and the boys in a slender volume called *Cannery Row* and it was seven years ago that he returned to the scene in a book called *Sweet Thursday* (naturally the day after Lousy Wednesday). "I can never go back to Cannery Row in a literary sense," Mr. Steinbeck told us the other day over a glass of beer in the study of his home on East Seventy-Second Street. "Those people are dead now, and the place itself has changed. It's full of restaurants and tourist attractions. Doc's laboratory has been turned into a sort of genial drinking club, with electric guitars and all that sort of thing. I've never been in it but maybe I should. Come to think of it, Ed Ricketts would have loved it, so what am I beefing about? He was Doc."

We asked Mr. Steinbeck how the Cannery Row books rated in his own estimation among the twenty-five novels and plays he has written, and he promptly disowned any feeling of affection toward any of his work. "The books are a record of the things that happened there and that's all," he said. "I liked the people. It was a crazy place. But I have almost no feeling for a book after it's finished." He drained his glass of beer and filled it again. "I like beer," he said. "Once in Monterey the boys had a birthday party for me. It was a wild and raucous thing that went on for three days and nights. Each man had five gallons of beer to drink. It was the second night, or maybe the third, that Ed Ricketts took a big swig of beer and lay back on the bed and went to sleep. He slept about twenty minutes, certainly no more, then sat up and took another big jolt of beer. He wiped his mouth with satisfaction and announced to us, 'There's nothing like that first taste of beer.'"

A deep-voiced, blue-eyed man with a thick beard and a thinning head of sandy hair, Mr. Steinbeck told us he was a rapid writer but that he invested tremendous amounts of time in preparation. "I wrote *The Grapes of Wrath* in one hundred days," he said, "but many years of preparation preceded it. I take a hell of a long time to get started. The actual writing is the last process. The first draft of my latest book, *The Winter of Our Discontent,* was completed between March 15 and July 10 last year, but the preparation, false starts, and waste motion took two and a half years. I have taken as much as six years to prepare a book for writing. There is such a delirium of effort in the production of a book; it's like childbirth. And, like childbirth, one forgets the pains immediately so that when you come to write another one you dare to take it up again. Some precious anesthesia sees you through. I've done so much of it now that I really don't know how you do it, and it's not terribly important to me anymore."

At the door, he told us he was leaving in a couple of days for Barbados where he expected to spend at least three weeks. He gazed at the snow piled against the curb in front of his house, and said, "There are grapefruit rinds under that snow that they won't find until July."

A TALK WITH ALFRED BESTER

Not long ago the Franklin Institute in Philadelphia gave a party at which algae were served as refreshments. Algae, in case you don't recall the word at sight, are the little one-celled creatures that make up the green scum on still ponds and swamps but which are so packed with nutrients that just about everybody agrees they will constitute the primary item of diet for space travelers. We missed the Franklin Institute party—a statement containing not the slightest trace of regret—but we have just had a talk with Alfred Bester, a distinguished science-fiction writer whose *The Demolished Man* stands as one of the classics of that field, with the result that we now feel right on top of the subject. An erect, handsome man with a distinguished-looking beard and a piercing gaze, Mr. Bester said that such things as space travel and nuclear fission were old hat to science-fiction writers who, for years, have been working with these subjects. "I was directing a Charlie Chan show on NBC when news came in about the explosion of the A-bomb over Hiroshima," he recalled. "Everybody in the studio got terribly excited about it. I have been living with this thing for twenty years, so I said, 'Let's get on with the rehearsal.' They thought I was made of stone. Rockets to the moon, satellite rockets in orbit—these things are so old to science-fiction writers that the fact that they are really happening now doesn't interest us. We knew all along these things could be done if someone put up the loot to do it. The tragedy of science is the fact that money for exploration is not made available until some military value is proven, as radar was developed in England."

What about algae, we inquired. "Oh yes," he said. "Well, in the first place, eating in space is going to be absolutely dreadful. Travelers will probably eat yeast cakes made of algae, which are neither animal nor vegetable, but half of each. They are packed full of goodies as far as nutrition is concerned, but the taste is horrible. The government is doing research now on what no-gravity will do to the human being, but they haven't yet gotten around to determining what an algae cake diet will do. There's no doubt about it, though, pound for pound, it's the best concentrated food available, and if you are out in space for a long time you can grow it in tanks. Imagine, reaching out to scrape your breakfast off the side of a tank."

While we were imagining this, Mr. Bester took a deep breath. "In fairness to the government," he went on, "the reason that very little experimentation has been conducted in the field of null-G cooking—that's a term for 'no-gravity'—is that it's almost impossible to create null-G. The best way to do it is to put a plane in a very steep dive, and for about nine seconds you almost have null-G. But what in hell can you cook in nine seconds?"

We asked Bester if he were doing any writing, and he said he was working on a novel about Fire Island. "It's based on a gimmick the late Woolcott Gibbs told me," he said. "It's a wonderful device, and Gibbs assured me he never intended to use it himself. I was afraid he would tell some *other* writer about it, so I kept asking him if he had told anybody. When he finally said, 'Told what?' I began to feel safe."

A TALK WITH ROBERT GRAVES

Robert Graves, the British author, poet, and classicist, was in this country recently on a lecture tour, and a few days before he left New York to sail back to his home on Majorca, we tracked him down at the apartment of his daughter to ask his views on current literary matters as well as to put some questions to him about life in the international world of letters. A towering, white-thatched man with a ruddy face and an air of authority, Mr. Graves received us graciously and said that he would speak with candor on any subject we cared to introduce. "As a matter of fact, I've done little more than talk, talk, talk since I've been here," he said. "I must say that Americans are good listeners. I've given two readings and several talks. I spoke at Johns Hopkins in Baltimore several days ago and in Washington yesterday. This is a fine break in the winter for me, because there is no sun in Majorca at this time of the year and it's very damp there. While it's colder here, the houses are all well heated and I like the change."

Feeling it was time to get down to business, we asked Mr. Graves how he classified himself. "I am primarily a poet," he said firmly. "My whole life has been geared to that fact. The interminable problem facing the poet is how should he support himself, and the first rule seems to be that he should have no boss. When I left the army in 1919 I decided to be nobody's stooge. I was offered a job at the Royal Egyptian

College, which I took because my wife's illness required a hot climate. I soon left the job. Ideally there are all sorts of jobs one can take and be a poet at the same time, and I have tried them all and they all have disadvantages. Now, like the man who breeds dogs because he likes cats, I write prose. I find great difficulty in settling down to write poetry; a poem has got to *occur*. I've also learned that poetry is apt to occur in the intervals between prose jobs—a sort of secretion which manifests itself between jobs."

We asked Mr. Graves to say something about his books and he accepted the invitation with what appeared to be relish. "I wrote a book called *The White Goddess*," he said, "which states the position of the poet and traces the historic implications of the poetic seizure. To compensate for that, I did a close historical study on Christian origins. This book, *The Nazarene Gospel Restored*, is used subrosa in certain theological departments of American universities. There is a tremendous taboo against exposing real origins of the Gospels, even though Jesus comes out of it rather better than the Gospels. I found it almost impossible to get a hearing because all reviewers of theological books are clergymen. I have written eight historical novels, and they were more history than novel, really. I wouldn't write a *Forever Amber* which is a historical novel. In *They Hanged My Saintly Billy* I went very deeply into the history of Dr. William Palmer and I proved to my satisfaction that although he was a terrible wretch he did not commit the crime for which he was hanged. Dr. Palmer had been injudicious enough to antagonize the police, the insurance companies, and the Jockey Club so he hadn't a chance. Over here, "Playhouse 90" converted the book into a television drama, and I was distressed to find in this version, Palmer was guilty. I should add, too, that one of the sponsors was an insurance company."

We wondered aloud if Mr. Graves was doing any work, other than giving talks, while he was here, and he laughed heartily as though the idea was too preposterous to discuss. "Oh my, no," he said. "I can't write in America."

WILL SUCCESS SPOIL
SLIM AARONS?

We thought it had been a big year for Slim Aarons, the photographer, at least so far as we were concerned, but a glance through our notes showed that for years he has been popping up as the principal of some bizarre incident and always with the same look of bruised innocence that an Apalachin defendant would show if handed a parking ticket. Well, Aarons did it again, this time in Rome, where he was shooting pictures for a magazine and an American film company was shooting a movie called *Bay of Naples* starring Clark Gable and Sophia Loren. The two photographic enterprises were independent, to a point, but they came together promptly when the producer of the movie offered Aarons what they felt at the time to be a small part in a scene with Gable.

Accounts vary, but observers who were in Rome at the time all agree that Aarons had one line to say: "I'm in the laundering business, cleaning up." Not a fat part, surely, but a speaking part. Nothing much happened the first day, according to reports. Aarons sat around topping Gable's jokes. The next day he was handed a script and told to rehearse with two other people who were to appear in the scene. Gable's mounting uneasiness over losing out in the scene is said to have diminished sharply at that time. "I feel better," Gable was heard to mutter to an associate. "I've heard him rehearse."

When the time arrived to shoot the scene, Gable delivered his line and looked at Aarons. "I'm in the cleaning business," said Aarons, "laundering up." The director suggested they shoot it again. "I'm in the laundry, cleaning up," Aarons said. "Try it again," the director said pleasantly. "I'm cleaning up in the laundry," Aarons said, a little wildly this time. "No, I'm in the business, cleaning up. I'm in the cleaning . . ." Fifteen takes later Aarons got his line right, and the company was dismissed for the day. There was less than five hundred feet of film on hand, and Gable said he thought he's like to lie down for a while.

Aarons, currently, is between pictures.

A TALK WITH
JOSEPH WECHSBERG

If you happen to be driving around Vienna this winter and come upon a Buick bearing a hand-painted Connecticut license plate and an impressive-looking gentleman in his early fifties, the chances are that you have encountered Joseph Wechsberg, the well-known writer, musician, and gourmet, who has settled down in the Austrian capital but who stubbornly refuses to sever his ties with Redding, Connecticut. We had a drink with Wechsberg recently in New York, shortly before he boarded the *Liberté* to return to Europe, and we couldn't get over the feeling that this was the way a writer should look: suave, worldly, self-possessed. "I was born in Czechoslovakia in a village called Moravska," he told us obligingly, but with considerable accent. "I studied at the Vienna Conservatory of Music, I was graduated from the Sorbonne in Paris, and later attended the Prague University Law School, which, of course, is in Czechoslovakia. Now I live in Vienna, which is a fine place because it has good music and the mountains are nearby. I'm very fond of mountains. I have a small house in Heitzing, a nice, quiet section and an ideal place to write stories. It's a very modest house by American standards, but it makes no difference to me how many bathrooms you have as long as you're happy. Am I right?" We assured him that he was, and he resumed:

"I live what you call a split-personality life. When I think of Redding, it breaks my heart. I would like to have an American home but live a Vienna life. I miss the people in America. My wife painted our Connecticut license plate and it's probably the only hand-painted license plate in Connecticut. Certainly it's the only one in Vienna. I was tempted to take a snapshot of it and send it to the governor."

Wechsberg came to America in 1939 and became naturalized as a soldier in the U.S. Army. "I have done many things," he said. "I have been a writer, a musician, a lawyer, of course, a salesman, a croupier—I scarcely recall them all. So far as my writing is concerned, I'm now trying to get away from food pieces because I don't want to be typed as a food writer, and it's so easy to become typed in this country. I really prefer to be known as a reporter. Let me put it stronger: I am proud to be a reporter—it's a very difficult business. In many countries honest reporting is impossible, but here it is possible and I'm thankful. I travel a lot, but mostly in Europe and Africa. I speak German, English, French, Czechoslovakian, Italian, and Polish."

Although he has written widely about food, Wechsberg said his own tastes are simple. "Good food is simple food," he said firmly. "The hamburger and baked Idaho potatoes that you have in America are good. When I'm working my lunch seldom consists of more than a sandwich and a cup of coffee. I'm a terribly slow writer and I seem to be getting slower all the time. This is because of endless rewriting and the fact that I'm never satisfied. I'm terribly pleased when people tell me that my writing appears light and unlabored. I try to keep hours. I start work around eight o'clock and what I haven't done by one o'clock is likely to be no good. I read during the afternoon and I've now reached a point in life where I can afford to be a selective reader. At fifty-two, that's a compensation."

BUCHWALD TAKES THE STAND

Art Buchwald, for years the New York *Herald Tribune*'s Paris columnist, cornered Ted Patrick during one of the latter's forays into the French capital a few years ago and wrung a column from him on the travails of a magazine editor. We brought the situation to a full circle, as the saying goes, when we cornered Buchwald a few weeks ago in the bar of the Hotel California, just across the street from the *Herald Tribune*'s Paris office, and put a few questions to *him*. A stocky, thirty-three-year-old chap with a slightly melancholy

air, Buchwald told us that at the time he interviewed Patrick
his column almost always followed the interview pattern. "It's
changed now," he said. "I still do an occasional interview but
more often than not it's a straight humor column. Interviews
are difficult to bring off, especially in seven hundred and fifty
words, which is all I have to work with. Generally, I interviewed celebrities, and the trick, of course, is to get the person
to stick to one subject and not ramble. Writers as a class are
good subjects; you can pick out a subject and kick it around
with them and always end up with something. Patrick talked
intelligently, but generally I steer clear of editors. Steinbeck,
Hemingway, and Jim Thurber were great. The worst of all
are movie stars who haven't a damn thing to say—except
fellows like Frank Sinatra or the late Humphrey Bogart.
Crackpots from the international set are good too because
they don't mind making fools of themselves. The most un-
funny people of all to interview are comedians; they can't
think of anything amusing to say and usually are very boring."

Buchwald has no sympathy for the humor writer who claims
it is impossible to satirize anything in America now because
of the sensitivity of editors or advertisers. "Too many humor
writers in America spend all their time bewailing their inability to be funny," he went on. "This is absurd. Knocking
hell out of the big guy has always been funny and still is.
Take the controversy I got into over the Jim Hagerty matter.
I spoofed Hagerty in my column and he blew up. He is a
pompous little man who can't take a joke. I got two good
columns out of it by just giving him the needle. But another
thing humor writers should remember in their moaning over
their fate is that satire has never had a very wide appeal. It
needs an intellectual—not a mass—audience. I don't think the
audience for satire is any smaller now than it ever was."
Buchwald acknowledged that for a humor writer and columnist he is in an ideal position in that he is separated from the
majority of his readers by the Atlantic Ocean. "This insula-
tion by distance," he said, "prevents people from picking up
the telephone and saying 'I'm mad because of your yesterday's

column.' Also, there's the feeling in the United States that I'm European and Europeans are likely to do anything."

The Buchwald column, which is now printed in fifty-five newspapers in the United States and thirty abroad, takes slightly less than two hours to write, although the author may have been tossing the idea around his head for two days or more. "I'm not five minutes ahead with the damn thing," Buchwald said ruefully. "Always there's a deadline staring me in the face. I'm working on a new novel now—my last was called *A Gift from the Boys* and was published by Harper's and sold to Columbia Pictures—and that presents a problem. I may be going hot on the novel but suddenly I see it's four o'clock so I have to put the book away and start on the column. I'd like to get some money stashed away so I could loosen up and stop trying to write what I think is salable and write what I want to write. I learned a lot from the last book, which got pretty fair reviews. It took me a full year to write it, and I was constantly aware of the fact that I was strictly on my own—that I had no publisher close by to encourage me. I missed that, but it's one of the things I will have to get used to as long as I live and write abroad." He looked at his watch, and started to get to his feet. "I've got to get across the street and get started now," he said. "I haven't an idea in my head. Jim Thurber is in town and maybe I'll call him this afternoon. He's always good."

A TALK WITH TRUMAN CAPOTE

Truman Capote (pronounced Ka-poh-tay) is a deceptively drowsy, small young man with light hair, even features, and blue eyes which range in expression from mischief to outright malice. In the past ten years, he has described a wide arc across the nation's literary firmament, contributing novels, short stories, reportage, drama, motion-picture scripts, and just about everything a writer could produce, with the exception of verse. Now he has settled down to a humdrum sort of existence involving little more than two or three trips to Europe a year and whatever work is involved in writing three books. Once, a few years back, we tracked him down at the Colony Restaurant, where he frequently dines when he ventures across the river from Brooklyn into Manhattan. Wearing a gray nailhead suit, pink shirt, and bow tie, which, for the Colony, is practically protective coloration, he was smoking a cigarette and chatting with friends at an adjoining table when we joined him.

"The 'e' in my last name is pronounced," he told us when we hesitated a moment over it. "There was a song in the musical show *Flower Drum Song* which used my name and they didn't pronounce it correctly. It made me furious when I heard it. I expect to do a magazine piece about an island off the coast of Greece. The island is called Paros, and I spent most of the summer there this past year. I usually go to Europe two or three times a year, but I went there four times last year. I can work well there. My book *Breakfast at Tiffany's* (Random House), was bought by Paramount. I did not do the film script for two reasons of just about equal importance: I am not interested in writing films, and, secondly, I always like to go on to something new. Actually there is no place for the writer in the current Hollywood setup. The way films are made now, a writer is expendable. I did one film—with all the freedom in the world, incidentally—and it was great fun. It was called *Beat the Devil*, and I thought it turned out to be very funny."

Mr. Capote received, with considerable grace, a trio of acquaintances who paused at his table to pay respects, and then continued. "I've made the mistake of writing for the theater twice," he said. "I converted my novel *The Grass Harp* into a play—a play, incidentally, which I still like. I also wrote the book of a musical show called *House of Flowers*. If I ever write anything for the theater again, it will be an original play. I am very much interested now in writing reportage. No one has explored this area, which I think embraces a real art form. A few years ago I wrote an account of the *Porgy and Bess* tour to Russia, and more recently I did a reportage of Marlon Brando. Dorothy Parker wrote a piece about me and she said I had three gears: those of a novelist, a short-story writer, and a reporter. I would like to be a good writer in each of those forms. I am getting together a book of reportage now. A piece on Brooklyn will be in it, as well as the Brando article and seven or eight others."

We asked if his working day was a long one, and he paused as if trying to recall. "I work about four hours a day," he replied, adding that at least an hour and a half of that time was wasted. "I work better in the afternoon or evening," he went on. "I read a lot, averaging about six books a week. I always write in longhand, and I always rewrite three times, even though ultimately I may not change a word of what I have written. The second draft goes on such horrible yellow paper that I couldn't turn it in, even if I were satisfied with it. Then I type it, and this is the third draft. I plan very carefully what I am going to write. In doing reporting, I never take notes. The kind of reporting I do makes note-taking impossible, as the subject becomes self-conscious and freezes up. I find I have an audio-photographic memory and can remember anything I'm told for as long as ten hours. When I say I remember a conversation verbatim, I mean *really* verbatim right down to a slur of the voice or intonation. I listen for about a half an hour to catch the subject's rhythm before I start recording."

A lady stopped at his table and told Capote she had heard a great deal about his Brooklyn home and would like to see it. "Come and see it," he replied pleasantly.

A TALK WITH
ARTHUR C. CLARKE

With several satellites orbiting around our star, it struck us as a fine time to have a talk with a former chairman of the British Interplanetary Society, a former chairman of the International Astronautical Congress, and one-time chairman of the Symposium on Space Flight at the Hayden Planetarium, and when these titles are all held by one man, it becomes even more compelling. The man is Arthur C. Clarke, a native of London but now a resident of Colombo,

Ceylon, and we caught up with him at the Hotel Chelsea, in New York, as he was poised to take off on a lecture tour which would require him to eat creamed chicken in forty-one American cities. A restless, ruddy man of forty, with a standard British accent and inflection, Mr. Clarke kept up a steady stream of conversation, despite a constantly jangling telephone and a variety of interruptions.

"I've only been here a week and I'm still trying to get my appointments in order," he said apologetically, waving at the telephone. "This visit will last four, perhaps five months altogether, but most of it will find me on the road filling lecture dates. I have three lectures: one is on science fiction, one on space travel, and one on the earth-satellite program. All can be given with or without slides. There's no need to tell you that these are pretty hot subjects right now. People frequently ask me how I can learn about these things without colliding with security precautions, but security is no problem with me whatever. The only really secret thing about missiles now is the guidance mechanism, and I'm not concerned about details. My interest is in general principles."

Rummaging through a valise, Mr. Clarke lifted out an armful of books and tossed them on the bed. "Although I lecture a lot," he said, "I'm primarily a writer, and anything else I do is peripheral. To be more specific, I'm a writer on science and scientific subjects. Fact and fiction are of equal importance to me. Underwater exploration is the next closest thing to my heart, and I've written a lot on that subject." He held up copies of *The Reefs of Taprobane* and *The Coast of Coral*. "These are books I have done on that subject," he continued. "Harper & Row publishes all of my nonfiction, and Harcourt, Brace & World publishes my fiction. My last book of science fiction, *The Deep Range,* was based on my experiences on the Great Barrier Reef and dealt with whale ranching. Whales should be treated like cattle, which they are. I made the point that it's time agriculture moved to the sea where it belongs—but that's a subject I could talk about all day."

Clarke had been ignoring the telephone, but now picked it

up and talked at length with someone whom he later identified as one of his publishers. "People are amazed when I tell
them I'm staying at this hotel," he said, "and most of them
never heard of it. Dylan Thomas had this very suite when he
went on his last beer binge. He went from here to the hospital, and he died there. By the way, would you like a beer?"
We said we guessed not.

ARTHUR C. CLARKE REVISITED

Arthur C. Clarke, the author–skin-diver–outer-space
expert who has been free-associating on paper for the past
few years for the benefit of the more forward-looking readers,
is a pink-cheeked, springy, highly articulate man of middle
age who appears willing to accept the good living that this
planet—or any other—has to offer. Learning that he was back
in New York, resting up before setting forth on a lecture
circuit, we dropped around to the Hotel Chelsea, his West
Twenty-third Street headquarters, to see what had been
learned recently about the moon and the nearby planets.
"Absolutely nothing," he said, pushing a collection of books,
magazines, and pamphlets from a chair and asking us to sit
down. "Astronomers have had no interest in the nearby planets for the past fifty years. They know all there is to know
about them. So far as the moon is concerned, astronomers
couldn't care less. It has no real secrets."

What, then, of travel to the moon? we asked Clarke. Is that
imminent? "I fully expect to go to the moon myself, within
the next twenty years," he said matter-of-factly. "In all prob-
ability, some magazine will send me there on assignment.
Suppose thirty years ago someone had told you that planes
would be crossing the Atlantic Ocean in six hours, would you
have believed it? Possibly not. There is no longer any question of man's being able to stand the elements on the moon.
Of course he will have to be insulated from them, but he
will soon develop techniques so that we can do what we want
to there.

"There will positively be human beings on the moon during the nineteen sixties. I think if the Russians decided on a crash program—and they are ahead of everybody right now, make no mistake about that—they could do it in five years. They can do it *easily* in ten years. Their last shot could have gotten a man to the moon, but of course he couldn't have gotten back. Men will be flying around the moon easily in the next ten years, not just landing there. What we will do— and by that I mean earth people—is land robots on the moon before we actually send human beings there, and have the robots collect samples of all kinds. This will enable us to learn a hell of a lot about moon dust and the physical nature of the moon before we actually land there."

Since the moon seemed so elementary as to bore Mr. Clarke, we asked him what space problems were now occupying the attention of the astronomical community. "The big problem of the future," he said cheerfully, "is not how to get to the planets but planetary re-engineering after we get there." We must have looked puzzled, because he went on quickly. "This involves changing the orbits of certain planets to bring them closer to the sun and thereby improve their climate as well as make available new sources of energy."

The approaching lecture tour, he advised us, would be his last. "Not that I'm talked out," he said, laughing at the thought. "Lecturing interferes too much with my writing. Besides, it makes things work out badly. I spent the winter here and will spend this summer in Ceylon, where I live. This isn't a good arrangement. I have two full years of writing lined up, not including, of course, a book which Harper's will publish in June under the rather Toynbeean title of *Challenge of the Space Ship.* Most of my Holiday articles will be in it. Incidentally, I've done so much writing about the moon that a science-fiction writer has attached my name to a crater on the moon's surface. It's called Clarke Crater, but it's a highly fictional one. There are over seven hundred approved names to geographical locations on our side of the moon, and there will undoubtedly be that many or more when we get a look at the other side. So we'd better start thinking up names."

A TALK WITH RICHARD BISSELL

A few years ago, right after he had turned his best-selling novel *7½ Cents* into the best-selling musical comedy *The Pajama Game,* we called on Richard Bissell and later duly deposed that we had never seen a man more content with life. Well, a few days ago we ran out to Rowayton, Connecticut, to have another chat with Bissell, and we found him unchanged. Things are still going nicely, and he has the confident air of a man who isn't worried where his next million dollars is coming from. Since we last saw him he had written most of the script of *Damn Yankees,* had turned out another best-selling novel, *Say, Darling,* and had affixed his name to a contract to convert, with his wife's collaboration, the latter work into a comedy with music.

"I've gone out of the pajama business," said Bissell, a stocky young man with a shock of black hair, a neat mustache, and a quick laugh. "We closed down the H. B. Glover Company, of Dubuque, Iowa—that was my dad's company. I was superintendent before I got mixed up in this writing game. That sign on the wall in the next room that says 'Superintendent's Office' came off the pajama factory. I ripped it off when we shut down. Since I've been writing, I've done four novels and one nonfiction book. I like fiction better than anything else, and especially better than writing for the theater. The theater makes you buckle down to the rules. I didn't want to have anything to do with writing a show again, but here I am now working on this play for Jule Styne. My wife and I have done a preliminary outline of the action, and have split it up into acts and scenes. We met Styne last week, and he thought we had made a good start, so now we begin on dialogue. It's a straight play with music. No choreography. We may have a piano player in the pit, who will sit there and read his paper and smoke, and start to work when one of the characters has a song to put over. It'll be close to *Say, Darling,* you bet. I had never met Styne before, but I was taken by his ideas, which are very original. Actually, he charmed me into this job."

A young girl entered the room with a plateful of cookies, and Bissell introduced her as his daughter, Anastasia. We looked startled. "It's on the level," he said. "She was named Anastasia before the play was written. We named her after a Polish girl who worked in the pajama factory. My wife and I thought it was a pretty name. I have four kids, and believe me, friend, they keep me held down. We took the whole bunch with us to Hollywood not long ago when I went out there to work on the screen play of *The Pajama Game* for Warner Brothers. I thought the picture business was fascinating. We lived for three months in a goofy theatrical hotel on Sunset Boulevard called the Chateau Marmont. Boris Karloff lived there, and my kids used to tiptoe by his door. They were scared to death that door would open." We asked Bissell when he had written a recent musical comedy piece for a magazine, and he said he had finished it last summer in—of all places—Dubuque. "I had been working on it for months," he said, "and I was visiting back home and had a little free time so I took it out of my briefcase to finish up. I showed it to Fred Griffith, one of the producers of *The Pajama Game* and *New Girl in Town,* and asked him what he thought of it. After all, I've only been in show business three years. Griffith read it and said 'Un huh.' That's the only thing show business people ever say about show business. They never think anything's any good. I'm glad the magazine liked it."

A TALK WITH ALAN MOOREHEAD

A few weeks ago we had the pleasure of dining with Alan Moorehead, the author of books and countless articles in magazines in this country, Great Britain, and Australia, which, incidentally, happens to be his home. A sleek, darkly handsome man of medium height and European manner, Moorehead was, at the moment of our meeting, showing considerable enthusiasm over his forthcoming book, and his forthcoming trip across the United States (which he has since completed and with which he is now flirting across his typewriter in the manner of all writers getting acquainted with an engaging though elusive subject). "I don't know precisely what to expect from America," he said. "In some ways it is a terribly *ugly* country. But it is exciting now because of its new role of being the most powerful nation on earth and not quite knowing how to handle it. You will, of course, have this knowledge as soon as you educate an administrative class equipped to take over the job we did, and which the French did. I don't intend to write just a travel article because travel doesn't sound exciting unless you wind up in a train wreck or an air crash, and I am not eager to achieve excitement by either of those means."

In regard to his future plans, Moorehead said he intended to return to London for a while and then move on to Africa. "I was in Africa four months this past winter," he said, "and I don't know how long I'll stay there this time. Perhaps a year, perhaps—and more likely—two years. I want to get material for a book on the animals of Africa. To me the most fascinating element of Africa is its animal life, and right now I am preoccupied by the great tragedy of the fact that the animals there are being wiped out—slaughtered by the herd. I tell you that when the animals of Africa are finished, Africa too will be finished. You wait and see. Anyway, I want to do what I can to help preserve them and there are, of course, others who feel the way I do. While I am in Africa, my wife is going to Italy to look for a house. London is too cold for me during the winter months, and I would like to be able to live six months of the year in Italy and six months in England."

We asked Moorehead if events in the Suez area required any last minute revisions in a writing assignment on the Middle East. "I wouldn't change a line," he said defiantly. "This is old hat for the Middle East. It's seen a thousand Nassers come and go. The more things change the more they remain the same there. Nasser supplied the world with a summer's entertainment, that's all. I feel it would be terribly rash to try to update an article like this. The central theme stands up all right—that with the departure of the British, a political vacuum was created and that sooner or later someone, some power from outside, had to come in and fill this vacuum. I

must confess too that I have a fearful psychological block in
going over a thing that I have once finished and put aside.
So far as the American piece is concerned, I am appalled by
the prospect of tackling such a subject. If only I could do
something else but *write*. Couldn't I just paint you a picture,
run you up a small model of the Statue of Liberty in pottery,
or embroider a few table napkins with Old Glory?"

A TALK WITH CLIFTON FADIMAN

The other day we cornered Clifton Fadiman, the old
inquisitor of "Information Please" days, on one of his rare
forays into town from his retreat in New Canaan, and put a
few questions to him about the *Party of One* essays that he
has been writing for some time. We were surprised to find
that time had mellowed him considerably from the days when
he needled John Kieran and Franklin P. Adams so mercilessly
on the airwaves, although he still is hardly what you would
call humble. A stocky, wavy-haired man in his fifties, with a
familiar, resonant voice, Mr. Fadiman told us that he has
written a number of essays and that he hoped to do a good
many more. "Without any mock modesty," he said, "I would
like to help revive the nineteenth-century tradition of the
familiar essay. I don't mean to imply that the essay is a
totally ignored form. There are other essayists, such as E. B.
White, Edmund Wilson, and the late Bernard DeVoto—to
name a few—but no one else is doing this systematically.
Hazlitt and Lamb, the great English essayists of the nine-
teenth century, met deadlines every week, and they wrote on
a variety of subjects. It is my theory that the familiar essayist
should be able to write regularly and that he should not be
afraid of any subject. The word 'essay' comes from the
French verb 'to try,' and it began with Montaigne who wrote
on almost anything that appealed to him. I try to do this in
my pieces, even to the point where I have selected some subjects which probably made the readers mad."

The ten years spent by Fadiman as moderator of "Information Please"—the radio forbear of today's quiz shows—gave

him a fairly reassuring view of the extent to which the popular taste could be ignored without inviting disaster. "I have spent many years of my life doing things that, if not contrary to current tastes, were certainly not part of them, either," he said. " 'Information Please' was really against the current of the time, but it caught on anyway. The essay form also seems to be bucking the current, but right now it appears that there are a number of people who like this sort of thing. A collection of my pieces was published recently in book form under the title of *Party of One* by World Publishing Company and already over sixteen thousand copies have been sold. That's tangible evidence. Actually, I am not certain that there is any such thing as a contemporary person or a contemporary writer, because we are all part of the past, and some of the tastes of the past must lie, just beneath the surface, in all of us. I am now part of an NBC television show called 'Conversation,' which, quite simply, features literate, intelligent conversation. This, too, is bucking a trend because the television public apparently wants the prepared rhythm of something like the 'Sixty-four Thousand Dollar Question.' Yet 'Conversation' has survived two years, to the surprise even of the network. From somewhere there has appeared an audience for this show."

Although Mr. Fadiman has assembled some collections and anthologies, and is an inveterate writer of introductions to other people's books, *Party of One* is his first book. "I hope to do a *Party of One* every few years," he said.

We asked Mr. Fadiman if he followed any definite work schedule in his writing, and he fixed us with a stern eye. "The surest way to be inefficient is to have a schedule," he said firmly, and for a moment we knew what Mr. Kieran and Mr. Adams had been up against in the old days.

A TALK WITH FREDERIC MORTON

Frederic Morton, the Austrian-born author of *The Rothschilds,* talked with me recently, mostly about his piece "The Lure of Flirting." Forgetting for the moment that he was not under subpoena, we threw the following questions at him: (1) Where had flirting reached its greatest state of refinement? (2) How do American males stack up as flirts? (3) How did he know so much about flirting, anyway? Heavily loaded questions, all of them.

Quick as a wink (if you missed that one, don't ask us to repeat it), we learned that flirting is now in full flower in France and Italy, and is coming into bud in Spain; that American males are still in short pants where flirting is concerned; and that the author of the article obtained his facts from observation rather than experience. This latter was acknowledged a little sadly, we thought.

"I have been in many countries," Morton told us, "and in all of them I was interested in how the sexes reacted to each other. Flirting is a major occupation in both France and Italy, and now the Spaniards seem to have taken it up enthusiastically. There is no age limit to this thing, but it has been my observation that the best flirts are not young people; their impatience destroys some of the subtlety of the sport. The American male is poor at it, very poor. Flirting is a joyful experience, but the American flirt is too pragmatic to savor its full flavor. I dislike saying this but I'm afraid the American male will never be a good flirt because he is too preoccupied with the final outcome of it all."

Shifting from flirting to Salzburg (a long step, incidentally, since, according to Morton, there is very little flirting in that part of the world), we learned that although Viennese himself, Morton had been to Salzburg many times, the most recent of which was last year. "Without a week at Salzburg in the prewar years," Morton said, "a middle-class Viennese could hardly qualify as a respectable bourgeois citizen. In the autumn he would go to the coffeehouses and comment to the effect that Toscanini was particularly good that year or that Bruno Walter was perhaps a shade off from his performance of other years. Salzburg was a part of the life of Vienna. I didn't awake musically until I was in my twenties, but the aura, the perfume of Salzburg colored my early life."

Returning to the subject of flirting, Morton said that he

was thinking of doing a courtship article as a logical sequel, and we couldn't resist the temptation to inquire if he intended to rest the series there. "I rather think that would be the end," he said, and we closed our notebook with a sigh of disappointment.

A TALK WITH BRUCE CATTON

We had, a while back, a leisurely talk with Bruce Catton, the Pulitzer Prize-winning author of *A Stillness at Appomattox,* as well as several other books about the Civil War, and learned that, in the opinion of this great historian at least, the public taste for Civil War reading will last another ten years, that lazy people work the hardest, and that it's just as easy to write three books as to write one.

These revelations came about in Catton's office at 521 Fifth Avenue, headquarters of American Heritage, an historical quarterly of which he is editor. A tall, gentle, scholarly man with a quick wit but the diffidence of the genuinely shy, Catton fits comfortably the public image of a historian despite his denial. "I was a newspaperman and government worker too long to take this new label seriously," he said. "I have stumbled across a good thing at a good time, and to that extent I've been an opportunist. I have always, or at least it *seems* always, been interested in the Civil War, and when I started out seriously to write a few years ago, it was natural that I should turn to the subject of my greatest interest. Destiny was solidly on my side because I caught the upsurge of interest in the Civil War just as it was on the rise. My timing couldn't have been better, although it was the last thing on earth I thought of at the time. I hope the appetite of the public for Civil War literature holds out a while longer, and I think it's good for ten years more. It's my subject, and when it's through I will probably be through too. That's a risk a writer must take who specializes in a single subject, but even so I think it's smart to specialize. A writer can't be an authority in too many fields."

Catton's then current activity in the Civil War field was

brisk. He had just turned in to Doubleday the manuscript of a book to be called *This Hallowed Ground,* and was about to plunge into the preliminary work on a three-volume series on U.S. Grant, to be published by Little, Brown and Company. And immediately upon completion of the Grant trilogy, Catton would come home to Doubleday with a three-volume history of the Civil War which the publishers planned to feature as a centennial history. Thinking in terms of three books at a time, a prospect that would have the average writer bawling hoarsely for an analyst's couch, leaves Catton completely unruffled. With the aplomb of a man who isn't worried where his next book is coming from, he plans to board a small steamer later this month and enjoy a leisurely cruise to Great Britain. While he is eager to see London, it is really the deck chair work that appeals to him the most. "I'm a very lazy man which means that I have to work hard," Catton said. "Right now I'm tired. The idea of snoozing in a deck chair for a couple of weeks is the most attractive thing I can think of."

We asked Catton how his life had gone before fame tapped him on the shoulder, and he said that it had been pleasant but full of work. "For many years I was a newspaperman," he said, "and there is no harder work. I sometimes wake up in a cold sweat, thinking that I'm back on a newspaper. During the war I was information director for the War Production Board, and for a few of the postwar years I knocked around Washington doing information work and enjoying long lunch hours in the taproom of the Hotel Washington. Then I started writing. Let me tell you a funny thing that has happened to me. I never got through college, but last year three schools gave me honorary degrees, and this year I am going to pick up three more. For some reason that brings me vast satisfaction." He looked as if it did, too.

A TALK WITH EDDIE CONDON

Jazz music, whether you know it or not, has as many forms, or techniques, as psychiatry, and with that we gingerly discard the metaphor. While some people may hold that a few varieties of the more progressive jazz forms would have meaning only to an alienist, we ask you to remember that you didn't read it here. There is New Orleans jazz, Chicago jazz, Kansas City jazz, *le jazz hot* of Paris, San Francisco jazz, Progressive jazz, and Heaven only knows how many combinations and varieties of these, and the supporters of each have nothing but praise for their music and nothing but contempt for the discordant trash of the other schools. Determined to learn what some of the noise (a figure of speech, friends, nothing more) was all about, we dropped into Eddie Condon's place the other evening to talk it over.

Condon, a guitarist and one of the world's great jazz musicians, is an earnest-looking chap of middle age, with sandy hair and light blue eyes. He greeted us warmly, led us to a table in a corner of his combination saloon and concert hall, and signaled a waiter. "Turk Murphy is creating a lot of commotion these days with his San Francisco jazz," Condon said. "I had a long talk with Turk last year when he was in New York, and I've listened to a lot of his records. He's authentic, so far as his background is concerned. He makes his music sound as much like New Orleans as possible, including the mistakes. Frankly, I find it a little monotonous. He plays two-beat music, like this." Condon tapped a rhythm on our arm. "It's just transplanted New Orleans stuff."

We asked Condon what kind of jazz his band played, and he shook his head negatively. "We play small band music here," he said, "and it's all unscored. It's just jazz. That number the fellows just finished is 'Sugar,' a thirty-two-bar standard song. There were three rhythms and three horns playing on it. If I had been up there with the guitar there would have been four rhythms and three horns. If the guys played it again right now, it wouldn't sound like it did then. If it was scored, it would." A nattily dressed man in a gray suit with a red tie walked by and Condon introduced him to us as Mr. "Wild" Bill Davison, his cornet player. Davison moved on into the bar. "Getting back to Murphy," Condon continued, "he's a nice guy and there's room in jazz for everybody. I just think he's taking us back to primeval days in jazz. I can understand why Brubeck and those kids want to go forward but what makes a young guy like Turk Murphy want to go back?"

Although Condon gives the appearance of a man about to become violently ill whenever progressive jazz is mentioned, he denies harboring any prejudice against any of the jazz forms and doesn't think any of them were born under the curse of original sin. "I prefer unscored music like my guys play," he admitted. "They can go anywhere and play anything. But if people like the stuff Turk is playing, then that's fine too."

We asked Condon if he didn't think it at least worth while —we chose the word carefully—that Murphy was recreating the music of Jelly Roll Morton and some of the other old-timers from New Orleans, since hardly a man is now alive who wasn't smitten at some time by those old rhythms. Condon weighed the question for a moment and then met it head-on. "Murphy's a nice guy," he said.

HE JUST KEEPS
JELLY ROLLING ALONG ...

The jazz world being what it is, we were fairly sure the final word had not been spoken on the subject of Turk Murphy, and, sure enough, it was no time at all before we were calling on Margo Terry Rieman, an attractive young woman who divides her time between writing mystery novels and managing Turk Murphy's Jazz Band.

"Condon says Turk plays two-beat music," Miss Rieman said, getting right down to business. "He does, but what of it? That musical feud has been going on ever since the boys came up the Mississippi River. Sometimes Turk's boys play a tango beat because a lot of Jelly Roll Morton's stuff shows the influence of the Spanish. But Condon shouldn't confuse the beat with monotony. Condon's boys have a repertory of approximately thirty-five tunes. Murphy travels with a library of two hundred and thirty tunes."

Condon's implication that New Orleans, musically speaking, was a plague spot also caused Miss Rieman to wince. "One of the most interesting things that Turk is trying to do," she said, "is to recapture the 'happy sound' of the early New Orleans music. His engagement in New York proved his success in this attempt. He made music that made people have a good time. One of the most gratifying things about having him here was the surprise and pleasure of the non-jazz people we lured to his opening. Not only did they return night after night but they brought their friends too, to 'have fun.' The record for attendance was held by a Bach-loving ad man who showed up sixteen times."

Miss Rieman also permitted some skepticism to tinge her remarks about the virtue which she seemed to feel that Condon attached to unscored music. "There are two sides to this argument," she said. "The great bands of the 'thirties—Goodman, Dorsey, Glenn Miller and the others—all used arrangements. Ellington always has. Goodman's greatest popular success was 'King Porter Stomp,' a Jelly Roll Morton composition arranged by Mary Lou Williams. And to go back even further in the history of arranged music, the greatest of them all in many people's eyes are the recordings that Jelly Roll made in the period between 1926 and 1930. Free improvisation among a group of musicians has its points, certainly, but what the 'free' boys scorn has equal, if not more, interest to the more educated listener."

Miss Rieman drew a deep breath, and then asked if we would like to know how Turk describes his own music. We nodded, and she continued. "Turk says it's an ensemble form of music that's not basically dependent on solos. The white bands use ensemble as a way to get into solos. The early Negro bands had a happy sound we try to get now. Each musician in Turk's band is forced to listen to the other, to embellish or add to what's being played. This boils down to an appreciation of one another, musically. The spirit of competition is nonexistent. And while we are on that subject of scored music, could I say one more thing? Did anybody mention to you the fact that many of the musicians who scorn 'arranged' music would be unable to read an arrangement, let alone create one?"

IMMEDIATE RELEASE

We've often wondered what it would be like if there were no press releases, and now we think we know. It would be simply terrible. We say this impulsively, having just read a press release on Walter R. Haman, former U.S. Secret Service Agent, which contained this straight-shooting paragraph:

"Mr. Haman was one of the very few members of President Roosevelt's detail who was assigned to the new group then responsible for guarding President Truman and accompanied him to San Francisco, Potsdam, Olympia, Washington, and on many trips to Independence, Missouri. He was Agent-In-Charge of one shift of the White House detail responsible for the protection of the President and his family when, on June 20, 1946, he resigned voluntarily to enter full-time Christian work."

A TALK WITH HARRY KURNITZ

We had lunch not long ago with Harry Kurnitz, the playwright and screen writer. In quick succession Kurnitz told us the best Italian food was found not in Italy but in Paris, that he hoped never to lay eyes on Hollywood again, and that he loathed actors. "Never forget," he said, "it was an actor who shot Lincoln."

A tall, bespectacled man, slightly stooped, Kurnitz talked as though he were putting together a scenario. "If it turns out that my show, *Reclining Figure,* made money," he said, "I will head back to Europe soon. I'll go to Klosters, in Switzerland. That's a wonderful place. I don't care for the skiing because, frankly, I'm afraid of it, but I like to walk. Last winter one of the skiers told me to get on the back of his skis and ride up to the top with him. It sounded like a good idea and I did, but when we got to the top I said, 'How in hell am I going to get down from here?' He was gone in a cloud of snow. I finally got them to take me down in the accident sled, which was so humiliating I jumped off before we got to the village. But what's the difference between an accident before it happens and one after it happens? Getting back to the show, though, I've found that the playwright's biggest job is to make the audience *think* you've got a hit. If they think it's a hit they start laughing as soon as they open the program. You even get laughs out of the straight lines. But if they aren't sure about it, the same lines won't budge them. Of course, movie writing is in a class by itself. You won't believe it but I was reading the script of a Biblical movie not long ago and one character said to another, 'Leave go my hand.' That's not Biblical talk, as I remember the Bible. Anything can happen in Hollywood. One day during the war a fellow comes into the office of a writer I know, carrying a little package. This writer's office is about the size of a small closet. He says, 'What's in the package?' and the fellow tells him it is an inflatable lifeboat for eight men. The writer said, 'Quit being wise and tell me what's in the package.' The fellow opens the package, pushes the button on the compressed air cylinder, and runs out the door. That boat backed the guy in a corner and we had to hack him out of there."

Kurnitz was interrupted by a waiter inquiring who had the veal. "Is that the veal?" Kurnitz asked, recoiling in what appeared to be genuine horror. "That's the chicken," the waiter said. "This is the veal." "Well when you ask who's having the veal," Kurnitz said testily, "nudge it forward. Hell, I wasn't even going to claim that." He looked across the table. "Let's see now, where was I?" he asked.

A TALK WITH MARIO PEI

Several years ago we recall reading a statement by Dr. Mario Pei, Columbia University's famous language expert, that a person could get along anywhere in the world if he had command of only eleven languages. Eleven languages, indeed! When we learned that Professor Pei had written a book, we seized upon it immediately as an excuse to hurry up to Columbia and put the question to him, face to face. Yes, he said, he recalled making the statement and, yes, it was true. He anticipated our next question and met it calmly. "I speak four languages," he said, "according to my definition of 'speak.' They are English, French, Spanish, and Italian. By 'speak' I mean that I can go into any of those languages right now with equal ease and facility. I can stumble around in thirty other languages, some live and some dead. I can do rather well in German, Russian, Latin, and Greek, of course, Sanskrit, ancient Egyptian, Hebrew, Gothic, Old Church Slavic, and some other rare languages. I would have no trouble making my wants known in Dutch, Portuguese, Japanese, some of the Scandinavian languages, even Arabic and Chinese. Languages fascinate me, and I am convinced that the story of languages is the story of civilization."

A heavy-set man with a handsome, jovial countenance and a ready smile, Professor Pei (it rhymes with May) speaks about languages with the calm authority of a man who knows what he's talking about. When we asked what was the most difficult of all languages to speak, he didn't hesitate a second. "Irish," he said firmly. "That's really tough. If you want to know which is the easiest language to speak, I would have to say that depended upon your native language. If you speak English, then you would find Dutch and the Scandinavian languages the easiest to learn because they come closer to English than any others. English now contains a number of words that have been lifted without change from other languages. 'Piano' and 'studio,' for example, are both Italian words, yet we consider them English. 'Yacht' is a Dutch word and 'halt' is a German word. You probably don't realize how many words from other languages have found their way, unchanged, into English."

When we asked Professor Pei how he happened to get into the language business, so to speak, he reflected a moment. "I'm a Roman by birth," he said, "and I came to the United States when I was seven. I had to pick up English in a hurry, and the differences between the two languages, even at that age, attracted me. In high school I took French and about four years of Greek, and that gave me two more languages. I had literary leanings, but I wanted to read French and German writers in the original. Well, the first thing I knew, the languages had taken the upper hand and the literature dropped off in the background. I realized I had begun to like language for language's sake. It's a fascinating subject, and I've written nine books about it under my own name, I've had a hand in the preparation of seven other books, and I'm presently writing three more. And I'm constantly running into language surprises." We asked what kind of surprises, and he paused a moment before answering. "Like a sign I saw on a London theater marquee," he said. "The sign was: 'Latest American Film—English Subtitles.' "

5

The Animal World

DOWN, BOY

Art Buchwald, the New York *Herald Tribune* columnist, recently devoted his space to a defense of the French poodle. (We recoil, even, from spelling it. Was there ever a more descriptive word than poodle?) Well, anyone who would defend poodles in the first place is an immoderate type who wouldn't know where to stop, and, sure enough, Buchwald went too far. He proceeded to attack boxers, who, as all dog experts agree, are the ultimate refinement of the species and perhaps, the noblest of all animals. The *Herald Tribune* can open up its pages to such questionable material if it chooses, but we feel a responsibility to rebuke him.

We own a boxer, a magnificent animal possessed of a sense of responsibility that obviously exceeds Buchwald's. Her day is an earnest one. Each morning she makes periodic checks at the barn to see if the cows are in good shape and contented, then wanders down to the creek to check on the water level—she started this during the drought last summer and the fear of another dry-up still haunts her—then she walks the fence lines, disciplines the cat and chickens where necessary, and throughout it all keeps a cautious eye on the incinerator. A few flying sparks on one of these gusty spring days and she knows she would have a bad situation on her hands. All of this, mind you, while the average French poodle is lying on a silk pillow with its hair still in curlers.

You all right, Buchwald?

CHACUN A SON GOÛT

A few mornings ago, while driving from New York to Philadelphia, we happened upon a scene that both startled and pleased us, and although it threw us into the position of having intruded upon the privacy of an individual, that intrusion in itself added some significance to the occasion. It was very early; in fact, the sun had just appeared but had made no headway in dissipating the mist that hangs at that hour of the day over the New Jersey meadows. Suddenly, to the right of us, we saw a woodchuck standing erect, his head tilted back while he breathed deeply, his eyes not yet cleared of sleep.

We got the picture instantly. He had awakened a little earlier than usual, and, leaving the family still asleep, he had tiptoed out for a breath of air and a look at the cars. Perhaps he had left the bath water running, giving it a chance to turn warm, and we had the feeling that he was not too pleased with the taste in his mouth. He spat reflectively, scratched the back of an ear with a thumb, and squinted at the sky. It was too late to sleep but too early to start work, and he was obviously enjoying the momentary need to do nothing. His glance at our car, we noticed, was a mixture of interest and contempt. Tearing up and down the New Jersey Turnpike at sixty miles an hour—No Parking Except for Disabled Cars —was a hell of a way to occupy one's time, he thought, especially now that the last warm days of fall were at hand. There was a small apple orchard in the field behind the road and the ground was littered with windfalls; moreover, hunting season was over a month away. The sum total of this was

Peace and Prosperity for any man with sense enough to add it up.

We followed him in our rear-view mirror, a voyeur unwilling to tear away our gaze. He grimaced at the earth-pounding roar of a tractor truck, stifled a yawn, and turned back to his burrow. It was going to be a warm day, and it might be smart to grab another little nap before things heated up; or perhaps some sound warned him the tub was about to overflow. Just before disappearing he gazed around, and for a second our eyes met in the mirror. We were impressed by the fact that his gaze was calm, steady, and good humored.

A few hours later, back in our office, we picked up a copy of *Application of Routh's Algorithm of Network-Theory Problems,* by William D. Fryer, and glanced at the table of contents. One of the applications, we learned, was finding common factors of polynomials and another was computing Sturm's function, but there our eyes began to glaze over. It *was* getting warm, and we wondered if it would be smart to grab a little nap before. . . .

THERE'S NO WORD FOR GOOD-BY IN DOG LANGUAGE

Cannes, France

If you don't like dogs, our advice is that you skip this piece entirely. Perhaps it's therapy for us, and in that light the need to write it will be understandable. The dog involved is our twelve-year-old boxer, a fine old matriarch who somehow managed to seize control of us when she was just a puppy and who has ruled our household with an iron hand ever since. To deny that a dog can maneuver human beings is as unrealistic as to deny the existence of the Rocky Mountains. There they are, and there, too, is Punchy: firm, judicious, and as unwavering in her principles as a Tibetan monk.

During the preparations for this trip, it must have been clear to Punchy that she wasn't to be included; yet she stubbornly refused to acknowledge the fact. Wandering from room to room, snorting disdainfully into the suitcases, she adopted an attitude of total indifference; yet all the while she was about as easy to overlook as the U.S. Capitol building lit up. At first it was obvious that she expected to come, then when she failed to detect the symbols of her inclusion (the packing of her diet supplement, her kidney pills, her cortisone, and her ear drops) she preferred to think it was to be nothing more than a weekend jaunt which she could profitably spend on a neighbor's couch. But the piling up of the suitcases soon dispelled that wistful notion, and terror began to creep into her eyes. The hour of parting, we both crumbled. At that moment, only the primitive attitude toward pets of Queen Elizabeth II stood between Punchy and Europe.

Although dogs generally like to travel, Punchy always seems to get more than her money's worth out of trips. There were the dozens of trips to Maine that we took together, just the two of us, where we always had to put up for the night at the same motel because Punchy took a wanton fondness for it and would tolerate no other. Twice we tried to interest her in another location, since her favorite was far from being ideally situated from the standpoint of halving the trip, but she was so unpleasant about the change that we decided that good personal relations overbalanced inconvenience, and we gave in. One night, we recall, she paced sullenly around the strange room for hours, making just enough noise to keep us awake. Even then, it wasn't the noise that really prevented us from sleeping; it was the knowledge that she was sitting there in the dark, pouting. A sensitive man can't sleep through that kind of situation.

While Punchy's dignity carries her through most travel difficulties, she looks to us to set things right in emergencies, and when we fail her it is more than we can do to meet her gaze. Once she shared our bedroom (or we shared hers; its hard to say which) on the Broadway Limited to Chicago, and the Pullman conductor ordered us to close the door so Punchy wouldn't wander down the hallway. "She might get out there and bite somebody," he said. When we remarked that she didn't bite, he said, "She's got teeth, hasn't she?" It was only after we had closed the door that we realized we should have said, "So have you." We should have said it but we didn't, and Punchy somehow knew we had let her down. It was a tense evening. Punchy crawled in bed with us, but didn't get *too* close (she has dozens of ways to register coolness), and we both slept fitfully. The next morning as we were leaving the train in Chicago we passed a Pullman conductor. Fixing him with a level gaze, we said, "So have you." He stepped back, licked his lips nervously, but said nothing. We decided later it was a different conductor.

Of all of our trips, though, the ones she likes best are those to Atlantic City. The Claridge Hotel there appeals to her enormously. She marches grandly into the elevator, nods sedately to the operator, then turns and faces the door. The quiet elegance, the salt air, the over-stuffed chairs all add up to an impressive total for her. The first thing we're going to do when we get back to the United States is to take her to the Claridge for a weekend. She's going to be cool, very cool to us, but if anything will thaw her out, it's the Claridge.

IT SHOULDN'T HAPPEN
TO A DOG OWNER

"The trait that sets dogs apart from all other animals that have been studied experimentally by psychologists is their willingness to work for a reward of a most intangible nature—the approval of the experimenter," says Defense Manual TM 10–396 (How To Train War Dogs). Substitute derangement for approval and we're willing to let it stand.

Since puppyhood our boxer has had nothing but contempt for civilian instruction. "Fetch the newspaper," we said one day after the paper boy had missed the porch. "No, no! All of it. . . ." Military instruction, we decided, was the only solution, and a few days later we wrote for TM 10–396.

The first exercise we taught her was Crawling On Stomach Under Fire. Following the instructions, we got down on the ground and started inching forward, commanding the dog to follow. We had got as far as the gate when our neighbor's voice brought us to a halt. "Pulling a fadeaway on the Little Woman?" he asked from the fence.

"No," we replied, crawling through the gate. "Just training the dog."

"What dog?" he asked. We glanced back quickly. The dog was asleep on the porch.

A couple of days later the dog had Bringing In The Casualty down cold. We volunteered to demonstrate the command to our neighbor, who agreed to be the Casualty. "When she tugs on your trousers, follow her quietly and with confidence," we shouted across the fence, the words fresh in our memory. "Don't startle or excite the dog while performing the command."

"Roger," our neighbor shouted, trying to appear military. He had been a pre-Pearl Harbor father.

We never did learn what went wrong. "Let go my pants," we heard him shout. "Call the damn dog! Help! Let go."

"Don't frighten him," we shouted. "He may get it confused with Guarding The Enemy." We were too late. There was an ear-splitting scream, and we saw his wife running from the house. As we told her afterwards, she shouldn't have brought the broom because the dog undoubtedly thought it was a gun and was convinced that he was up against the enemy infantry, and everything that happened after that was her own fault. She didn't answer us. She hasn't answered us at all now for over three months.

We demobilized the dog and sent the book back to the Defense Department. We're waiting now for Manual TM–490 (How To Treat The Enemy When Conquered). There's no sense in neighbors not speaking.

YOU CAN'T TEACH AN OLD DOG OLD TRICKS, EITHER

Last week when we were still at a low point and the memory of the incident continued to hover around, we

started to write this, more in the hope that an orderly reconstruction of events would liberate us of any sense of guilt,
however slight, that we may have accumulated over what
happened. This kind of guilt can calcify, something we
sought to avoid at all costs, especially since we felt that we
had no responsibility in the matter anyway.

To go back to the beginning, we were invited to enter our
boxer, Punchy, in a dog show. A nice, printed invitation arrived in the mail, and we think it's important to keep that
in mind in view of what later happened. "If your dog can't
qualify in the breed events," it read, "enter it in the obedience trials. Prizes for all classes." The invitation is on the
desk of our study, under the Washington Monument paper-
weight.

We arrived late—Punchy is ten now and there was a little
trouble getting her in the car, or getting her to do anything
else, for that matter, that she doesn't want to do—and we took
our places next to an Airedale and his owner, who were
getting in position for the obedience test. Glancing over the
field quickly, we could see it was in the bag for Punchy.
There were eighteen dogs in the test, or twenty if you cared
to count the two Dachshunds who were entangled in their
leashes. Their owner appeared more concerned about saving
their lives than winning prizes.

We were trying to get Punchy to stand up when the Airedale's owner made what we interpreted as an overt remark.
"Sure you're in the right event, friend?" he asked. "This is
the obedience test."

We laughed, looking at the Airedale. "I can see why you'd
like us to drop out."

"It so happens, friend," he said, "that this Airedale is one
of the best-trained dogs in—"

"Oh," we interrupted, "so it's an Airedale."

We could see he was getting mad. "What does it look like?"
he asked unpleasantly. "A Poland China hog?"

"It might," we grudgingly admitted, "if you cleaned it up
a little."

Punchy, sensing the cold war was warming up, sank her

teeth silently in the Airedale's shoulder and the yelp that went up was said to have been heard by reliable observers on the outskirts of Trenton, some distance away. When the judge rushed up to restore order, Punchy, by now obviously irritated with the whole thing, transferred her attention to the judge's thigh, which was handy, and a new sound blended with the howl of the Airedale. Somehow this appeared to be a general signal to the other dogs, and when we glanced back, after loading Punchy in the car, the dogs were in complete control. Our heart went out to one spectator who appeared to be cut off from his car by two Dobermans, working as a team.

Our wife telephoned us at the office today to say the Airedale's owner had called. We asked her what he wanted and she said she had asked him the same thing. All he had said was satisfaction and that he would come by tonight for it.

ALL THE NEWS THAT'S FIT TO PRINT INCLUDING RECENT PATENTS

Our hats are off to Mr. Harry C. Petrie, of Seattle, who has just been issued Patent No. 2,725,036! Mr. Petrie's invention is a polygamous breeding cage for chinchillas, and news of his good fortune reached us through a story in *The New York Times.* Polygamy is desirable in the breeding of chinchillas, we were told by the *Times,* but if the animals live in pairs the female, being the stronger, is likely to kill her mate. We now quote the *Times* direct and with no further comment:

"Mr. Petrie has designed for polygamous breeding a cage like a miniature four-story apartment house. The lone male lives in the central hallways, and becomes friendly with all the females, but through the bars. An attendant can open a particular door when he wants to promote mating. The runways in the hall are somewhat intricate, and only the male is familiar with them. If the female chases him with murderous intent, he can keep away from her, at least until the attendant comes to his rescue."

THE CAT HAS NO NATURAL ENEMIES?

We suppose cats are the most loathsome creatures ever to move across the face of this planet. Sly, cold, and cruel, they slink along alley walls and through hedges, the most merciless murderers of all time. To see a crouched cat, its belly hugging the ground, preparing to pounce on a bird or a field mouse is to witness an attack that by comparison would make Lizzie Borden's ax-work seem like a gentle act of self-defense. A cat is a loathsome animal and it should be sent back where it came from. Hell, most likely.

Fascinated by the total evil of the cat personality, we have spent considerable time in the past few years engaged in what psychiatrists would call a depth analysis of the cat psyche, and we have a few conclusions which, now properly evaluated, can be passed on to the public. In the first place there's not a felon in Leavenworth who doesn't have more honor than the noblest cat that ever lived. Cats actually *prefer* to steal. (See Experiment No. 23 in our raw notes, in which we detail the incidence of cats jumping on the table to get less desirable—from the cat viewpoint—food than was lawfully available on the floor.) Furthermore, we would like to erase the illusion that there is any such thing as cat loyalty; a cat will feign loyalty, but only long enough to learn where the silverware is hidden. One man is the same as another to a cat, unless, of course, one of them has something the cat wants. Then the cat enters down-stage and puts on a performance that for sheer winsomeness was never equaled by Mary Pickford.

We tolerate a cat in our home but only at the insistence of the female members of the household who lack our perception of cat villainy. We have recorded this cat's history of moral digression, and it's sordid, if lively, reading. She kills wantonly, betrays us (her beloved family) daily, steals for the sheer pleasure of the felony involved, and recognizes no law of God or man. Like all other cats she is grotesquely awkward (the existence of "feline grace" is the greatest hoax ever put over on an unsuspecting public) and one of the noisiest animals, pound for pound, alive. (The persistence of cat-lovers in perpetuating the "quiet as a cat" myth has so excited us that we are considering the preparation of a special monograph on the subject.) By day the cat worries a pencil or some metallic object against the baseboard until our nerves snap, and she makes the nights hideous with her caterwauling. Some pet.

There's one cat attribute that we have definitely disproved and that is the cat's ability to land on its feet. We have found, in throwing this cat down the cellar stairs, that if we give her, well, a certain spin, she will land on her head every time. Moreover, we will be glad to demonstrate this any time in your own home, with your own cat. No obligation of any kind.

HOLIDAY HOUSE

For some time now, reports have been reaching us about Holiday House, a sort of Greenbrier or Boca Raton for dogs located near Doylestown, in Bucks County, Pennsylvania, and which is described by the management as "America's finest boarding kennel." We were surprised to see the work "kennel" appear in Holiday House's official literature because we have been told that the pens were called apartments, the runs were called recreation areas, and the reception hall was called the commons. Moreover, we had heard that the pe-(sorry) apartments were equipped with indirect lighting, that the floors gave off radiant heat to prevent drafts, that linen was changed daily, and that there was a well-stocked library including some picture books for the very young dogs. We had discounted a report that the dogs were served only distilled water, and that on special occasions flowers were placed on the dinner trays.

Our boxer finished the winter a little depressed, and we decided recently to treat her to a couple of days at Holiday House with a view to freshening up her outlook and, incidentally, of giving us an opportunity to take a look at the place. Take our word for it, it's magnificent. There *is* radiant heat and indirect lighting, the apartments are floored with neutral tile, they are roomy and cheerful, and a friendly, holiday atmosphere exists in both the guest rooms and the commons. There is no distilled water, but each apartment has a built-in water bowl through which flows water, fresh from an artesian well, twenty-four-hours-a-day. Sick or convalescent dogs aren't allowed for obvious reasons. Get one or two dogs in there talking about their operations and first thing you know they all think they've got something. We didn't stay for either dinner (American Plan) or vespers (nonsectarian) because we had a long drive home. When we looked in on our boxer to tell her good-by, she was walking around the apartment, with a look of awe on her face, touching things. We stole away quietly.

WORKING CLASS

We've got another dog story for you. It concerns the characteristics of breeds. A few days ago we dropped in to an optician's, near our office, to pick up a new pair of eyeglasses. "What happened to your old pair?" the optician asked as he polished the lens. "Break them?"

"No," we replied, "my dog chewed them up."

"Boxer?" he asked.

We nodded our head affirmatively.

FOR THE BIRDS

One of the most appealing things about man is the stubbornness with which he insists that he is smarter than animals. That this conceit is exploded constantly by animals (who won't stay in a smoke-filled room, for one thing, or who refuse to let their work interfere with their sleep, for another) impresses no one; man goes ahead discussing his superiority in that wise, infinitely resourceful way that old fishermen use in talking to young boys. This subject was brought alive to us recently by *The New York Times,* which published the text of a cautiously-worded communique from the Mayor of Philadelphia claiming a victory in the city government's war against the thousands of starlings that roost nightly along the ledges and eaves of Philadelphia's City Hall. According to the *Times,* which is edited by men and therefore likely to be biased in its treatment of news of this kind, a Dr. Hubert Frings, of the University of Pennsylvania, broadcast recordings of distress calls of starlings on the theory that when the birds heard the distress sounds they would become frightened and fly away. Many did, thus affording the Mayor some basis for his victory statement. However, a couple of hundred remained, seemingly impervious to the week-long broadcasts, and it is the city government's contemptuous attitude toward these birds that has us emitting some distress sounds of our own.

"Dr. Frings believes that these holdouts must be mentally-retarded birds," the communique declared, "who don't know the meaning of a distress call. Or maybe they are deaf."

Well, we don't think they are backward, and we don't think they are psychos, and we don't think they're deaf. All the evidence given by the *Times* indicates that the holdouts saw through Dr. Frings's little scheme and felt there was no sense in pulling up old family roots and moving to a new town merely because of some phony recordings, which were rather low-fi at that. Our deduction was borne out a few days after the *Times* story appeared, when the Philadelphia *Inquirer* published a statement from Deputy Commissioner of Public Property Raymond J. Mauerman, who admitted that half of the original population of 100,000 starlings had returned. What had happened, of course, was that some of the smarter birds, who had refused to be taken in by Dr. Frings, had sent word to Camden and Chester that the whole thing was a hoax and that life at City Hall still offered all a starling's heart could desire, once you got used to those silly broadcasts.

The next move is up to Dr. Frings, and we say he's on the defensive.

6

At Home

Suddenly last summer, as we were driving back to town one evening after a day in the country, the realization struck us that we had never been a spectator at a drive-in movie. (There had been no such thing as drive-in movies during the peak days of our motion picture enthusiasm—a period presided over by Rod LaRocque, Vilma Banky, Esther Ralston, William Haines, and Nancy Carroll.) We had heard comedians describe the drive-in as "the place where you turn off the ignition and try the clutch" or "the place where the most gripping scenes are not always on the screen." We resolved to look into the matter, but what with one thing or another we still haven't got around to it. A brief news story in *Variety,* however, has just rekindled our interest and it will only be a matter of a few days before we can speak on the subject of open-air movies with the authority of an observer. The story follows:

Greensboro, N.C.—In Cleveland County a drive-in theater never advertises the name of the releases it is playing. The marquee always bears the same announcement: "Two Features."

Asked about this, the manager replied: "The people that come here don't care what's playing."

Moving on to another news story that engaged our attention, we would like to mention that at the time of the approaching trial of Adolf Eichmann, the former Nazi leader charged with complicity in the death of 6,000,000 Jews, we had read a very brief news account, practically buried on the inside pages, of the arrest of William Koppe, a former general in the Nazi S.S., who killed "only 300,000 persons." Surely in the Nazi scheme of things this is only a misdemeanor—a childish prank he committed during a moment when he wasn't thinking. But we sincerely feel that before dismissing Koppe, the court should tell him quite firmly that he should never do a thing like that again.

There's only one other matter we would like to discuss before letting go of your lapel. A recent wire-service story told of a parrot being brought into a Brooklyn court on a charge of using obscene language. The charge was brought by a Mrs. Amato, who testified that she walked three blocks out of her way each day to avoid "the parrot's stream of curses." Magistrate Harry Serper, of East New York Magistrates' Court, ordered the parrot brought into court. We now quote from the story:

"For two hours the parrot stayed there, blinking like a wise owl and saying nothing. Both the parrot and its owner were released for later trial on charges of disorderly conduct."

Now it's pretty obvious that Magistrate Serper ordered the parrot brought into court for the purpose of testifying against itself, which is not only underhanded but an out-and-out violation of the Fifth Amendment which secures for the parrot the right not to "be compelled in any criminal case to be a witness against himself." We would like to call this case to the attention of the American Civil Liberties Union, and at the same time announce that we have the honor to be the first to pledge one dollar to the parrot's Defense Fund.

CIVILIAN WAR

I think that I shall never see
The end of Joseph E. Johnston
  and Robert E. Lee.
And I would like to condemn
  to hell perennial
Whoever thought up the
  Civil War Centennial.
But at this stage it's useless
  to rave and rant,
Instead, I shall get quietly drunk,
  like U. S. Grant.

INSCRUTABLE EAST

From time to time we pass on to you stories dealing with the domestic *Sturm und Drang* of modern urban life, and we have one now that came to us recently from a well-known author who does a little lecturing on the side. He was recently asked to address a ladies' luncheon group on the subject of Chinese history and philosophy, and, although the Orient wasn't strictly his field, he did the best he could. As he was gathering up his papers to leave, he asked the program chairman why she had made China the subject for his talk.

"We wanted the subject to be appropriate," she said, smiling cheerfully, "because we were going to serve a chow-mein luncheon."

ARROWSMITH

The proprietor of a back-date magazine shop, where we occasionally stop to pick up an old copy of *Vanity Fair,* told us a few days ago of a visit he had had recently from a curious young man who had identified himself as a doctor and who asked for a selection of magazine "at least five years old." When asked by the proprietor if he wanted any particular magazines, the young doctor replied that he wanted some suitable for his waiting room.

"Look," said the doctor, confidentially, "if you had just started to practice, would you want all your patients to know it?"

NOT UNSINKABLE, UNTHINKABLE

We have been giving a lot of thought lately to the subject of musical comedies and we are now ready with our conclusion. They are so damned terrible it is difficult to discuss them seriously. We took a vow, awhile back, with our hand resting firmly on the Playbill of *Sail Away,* never to see another as long as we remain of sound mind.

It wasn't *Sail Away* ("One Million Dollars in Advance Orders," says *Variety*) alone that drove us to our resolution. It was *Sail Away* on top of *Let It Ride, The Unsinkable Molly Brown, Tenderloin, Fiorello, Wildcat, Saratoga, Redhead,* and—the way we feel right now—all the way back to *Blackbirds of 1928.* We can walk down the hall to the water cooler, whistling a song that we make up as we go along and for all you can tell it may be the hit song from any one of them. They are that dreadful.

The trouble, as nearly as we can tell between naps of fairly long duration, is that both the authors and the composers are following a master script from which they have sworn, under pain of being expelled from the Dramatists' Guild, never to stray. After having journeyed from Philadelphia to New York about twice a week for a dozen years or more, we have reached a state where we can look out the train window (we doze a lot on the train, too) and from a fleeting glimpse of the countryside tell precisely where we are. We have reached a similar state with musical comedies; we can rouse up for a moment and tell instantly, for example, that we are very near the scene where the madame takes all of the prostitutes to church, and, if we don't want to see the parasol-waving dance routine, we'd better drop off to sleep again quickly. We also know intuitively when the You're-the-Top-type song is due, this being a hilarious little number spangled with inside rhymes and making references to Las Vegas, Orval Faubus, atomic fall-out, and all those Kennedys. It's a forgettable moment in the American theater.

One question that has always perplexed us is how these shows, monoliths of tedium, manage to reach a stage, and that was answered for us a few nights ago on the wide walk outside the theater where *Let It Ride* was being given an out-of-town tryout. The show was over, the theater had emptied, and we were trying to think of something polite, if not encouraging, to say to the director. He appreciated our dilemma, and waved our comment aside. "When you get to this point," he said, "you've spent so much money, you're responsible for so many jobs, and there's so much company loyalty involved that you just can't walk away and leave it. You can't walk away and leave it."

Well, the audience has spent some money, too, and it has no way of knowing about those company loyalties. It's terribly easy, we're afraid, to walk away and leave it.

DEPARTMENT OF STATE
SPOKEN HERE

The language of diplomacy moves apace, its ken knows no compass. Our Washington man has passed on to us a fragment of conversation overhead in a hotel lobby in that city. One man, standing at an airlines reservation counter, said to another: "Don't mention his name to me. He's strictly persona au gratin."

UNION MEETING

A few days ago we dropped in at the annual meeting of the Authors Guild (what other publication takes you be-

hind the scenes and gives you a candid portrait of the col-
lective writer at work?), and our general impression was that
it resembled nothing so much as a meeting of Local 27,
United Mine Workers. The meeting, which was held in the
auditorium of the French Institute on East Sixtieth Street,
was scheduled to begin at two thirty, but at that time only
a small group had assembled. Most of the men were bald, we
noted, practically all of them wore glasses, and most of the
women were, to put it graciously, getting along. There was a
marked absence of grouping; most of the writers seemed to
prefer to sit alone.

At two forty-five, William L. Shirer, a tall, distinguished-
looking man, mounted the stage and called the meeting to
order. "Our president, Pearl Buck," he said, "is in Japan,
and God only knows where our vice-president, Cleveland
Amory, is. In their absence, I will preside." Before he had a
chance to warm up, though, Mr. Amory, who was taller even
than Mr. Shirer, arrived and took over. "Thank you, Bill,"
he said. "Let's have reports from the committees. We'll start
with John Hersey, who is chairman of the book committee."

Mr. Hersey, who was taller than anybody and who looked
remarkably youthful, reported that a new analysis of publisher contracts would be available shortly and predicted that
it would enable authors to get a better deal from their publishers. He sat down to a nice hand, the first show of life of
the meeting. In quick order the other committees filed reports. The membership committee said the organization had
1,849 active members; the junior book committee said it
wanted to change its name; the magazine committee acknowledged the loss, through death, of its late chairman, John
Lardner; and the Bulletin committee said the Bulletin spoke
for itself.

A lady arose to ask what was the attitude of the Authors
Guild toward book publishers who demanded a percentage
of movie sales. "We're against it," Mr. Hersey replied. That
seemed to settle that. "What is the attitude of the Guild
toward Bernard Geis Associates?" the lady asked. "We don't
take a position on any individual publisher," Mr. Hersey

replied. A male member observed that mystery writers felt that some royalty provision should be established in connection with rental libraries. "They rent one copy to two hundred readers," the member said, "but the writer receives only one royalty." Mr. Amory said that this deserved study. After a few more questions, Mr. Amory declared the business session ended, and turned the meeting over to a panel consisting of Hiram Haydn, John Brooks, Elizabeth Janeway, and Merle Miller. As the panel filed to the stage, we noted that they all wore glasses with the exception of Miss Janeway. We left a few moments later and were startled to see Mr. Amory a few steps ahead of us, carrying a briefcase and obviously in a hurry.

THE LONG CORD

We've just returned from Hollywood, where we spent a fitful fortnight, and from the moment we stepped from the plane we've been chewing our lip and brooding about the way the telephone has boldly enlarged its dominion over the people there so it is no longer the servant but the master of them all. This, then, is part rumination, part warning. For if, as we see it, the Los Angeles man is nothing more than a modern Laocoön, enmeshed in an extension cord instead of serpents, then those of us in the East who have found the long cord resistible should consider this a clear and present danger, and start mapping a defense. Oh, there are already a few table sets in some of the East Side restaurants of New York, but there is nothing like the long cord in Hollywood that trails from room to room, from room to porch, from porch to pool, and from pool to God only knows where. There is no place, so far as we could tell, from Santa Barbara to Long Beach that you couldn't receive a call, if you would only be patient, put your T-bird in neutral, and wait for the hand set to be fetched.

Even before our wonder at the long cord had subsided, we were introduced to a complex even more bewildering. This

is the growth of the answering service which, while not un-
known in New York, appears to have come to full flower in
the steamy canyons of Hollywood. If the tail fin is the status
symbol of the East, the answering service is the measure of
achievement in the West. Delivery boys, just like William
Holden, come home from a hard day's work and dial their
service to inquire what messages have piled up for them
during the day. The absence of messages is immaterial; what
is important is the service. A few words from the operator
sets the subscriber up for the evening and sends him jauntily
on his way.

The long cord is merely the umbilicus of Hollywood, a
native explained to us. He was patient because, being from
the East, we were not expected to catch on quickly. The
answering service, he conceded, was something else again and
more difficult to classify. "You know, don't you, that there
is a certain code of conduct, or manners, expected of all answering service subscribers?" he asked. We shook our head
negatively, and his manner bespoke his lack of surprise.
"Well," he said, "there is a very rigid code. The answering
service is really a hidden world of its own. For example, a
few months ago I had to go to the hospital, and on my first
day there I received flowers from four friends, none of whom
I had heard from in months. Do you know what had happened?"

Again we shook our head.

"I called my answering service and told them to send my
calls to the hospital," he explained. "The answering service
was under instruction from other answering services to report all people going to hospitals, since many of them have
standing orders from subscribers to automatically send flowers to certain names. So when my name showed up on the
hospital list, four answering services found they were under
instructions to send me flowers. The subscribers—*my friends*—
never bothered and actually never even knew I had been in
the hospital."

"What did you do about thanking your friends when you

got out of the hospital?" we asked. "Didn't that create a problem?"

He flashed us a patronizing smile. "Of course not," he said. "When I got out of the hospital, I called my answering service and asked it to thank my friends' answering services. There's a right way and a wrong way to do everything."

FIFTH GOSPEL?

We think it was Groucho Marx who once observed that some of the skepticism of the times may be due to the fact that "the Bible said one thing and Cecil B. DeMille said another." Well, we know now what DeMille *did* say, having just read "Yes, Mr. DeMille," by Phil Koury (Putnam). Now it befell that the author included a chapter entitled, "Matthew, Mark, Luke, John—and Cecil" and we recommend it, if only for the following story:

During World War II, while a blackout was in progress, DeMille went to the home of his neighbor, W. C. Fields, who at the time was not aware of the blackout, and, indeed, there was some authority for the belief that he was not altogether certain of the existence of the war.

"Yes, Mr. Fields, a blackout," DeMille said. "Turn off your lights and fill your bathtub."

"My God, Cecil," Fields cried, "can't we have a blackout without one of your bathtub scenes?"

PELMENYI AND BALLERINAS

Among the things we try to do from time to time is drop in on a restaurant that has been featured in a magazine or book to see if it's up to snuff and to judge for ourselves whether the writer had done a workman-like job or whether he had momentarily lost his head. With such a thought in mind, we called around at the Russian Tea Room, on West Fifty-seventh Street, one day recently and were lucky enough to run into both Sidney Kaye, the owner of the place, and

Silas Spitzer, who wrote a recent magazine article about it. The two were seated at a table against the wall, when we joined them, and Kaye was exhorting Spitzer to try the *Pelmenyi* for lunch. *Pelmenyi* is a speciality of the house on Wednesdays and, according to Mr. Kaye, at least ninety per cent of the people in the restaurant had specifically come for it. Not so Mr. Spitzer, who calmly disregarded the suggestion and ordered lamb chops.

"It's March, Sidney," Spitzer said. "When are you going to take down your Christmas decorations?"

"I'm early with the decorations for next Christmas," replied Kaye, a short, energetic man whose eyes roved the restaurant as though he were looking for someone. Phil Silvers, the television comedian walked by and Kaye smiled at him pleasantly. "There's a great guy, that Silvers," he said. "I told him the other day that his Bilko show was unusually good, and you would have thought I had given him a million dollars."

We asked what attracted show-business figures like Silvers to the Russian Tea Room, and Spitzer beat Kaye to the answer. "Where else can they get so much free advice as Kaye gives them?" he said. Kaye ignored the comment. "Mostly my customers are associated with the ballet or the concert hall," he said. "A lot of my business comes from Carnegie Hall. Sol Hurok comes here, and so does the head of the Ballet Russe de Monte Carlo. A lot of ballet deals have been cooked up here. In Harry Kurnitz' comedy, *Once More, With Feeling,* which is about a symphony conductor, Kurnitz has a character say 'May I forget an appointment with Jascha Heifetz and keep him waiting two hours in the Russian Tea Room if I'm not telling the truth.' Kurnitz is a good friend of mine and he comes here often when he's in town. But let me tell you something about ballet dancers. I've seen them sitting here, frail and delicate, waiting to be served and you'd think they couldn't get through a bowl of soup. But they eat like truck drivers. I've actually seen them eat their weight in food. I mentioned it to Hurok or someone in here one day, and he said a ballet dancer burns up as much energy in a five-minute ballet as a football player does in sixty minutes of play."

Kaye said he thought we should try the *Pelmenyi* and he signaled to a waiter and instructed him to bring us an order. "The same people keep coming here all the time," he went on. "I suppose this is a result of my father's instructions to me: 'First take care of your regular customers, then take care of everyone else.' A lot of people have found a home here. There's a man sitting over there by the wall who has eaten here every day for twenty-five years, and I have never even spoken to him."

"I've been coming here for twenty-five years," Spitzer remarked dryly, "and all I can say is that I'm filled with envy."

Kaye laughed. "Marlon Brando is an old friend of mine," he said. "He started coming in here when he was in *I Remember Mama*. The girls in the checkroom used to sew the buttons on his coat. The last time he came in he was wearing a plaid jacket and an ascot. When he saw me eying the ascot he smiled sheepishly. He's a very nice man, and I've always been very fond of him. William Faulkner started coming in about eight or nine years ago. I had handed out a little card asking my customers how they had happened to hear of the Russian Tea Room. One of them said, 'Word of mouth,' and was signed William Faulkner. He comes in very frequently. Most people come here because they enjoy the food. This isn't an elegant place in the fashionable sense."

"That's certainly true," Spitzer agreed.

"Spitzer is a good friend of mine," Kaye explained. "I'm fond of him, too."

FOR WHOM THE BELLE TOILS

The moral to this story is that you shouldn't skip any part of a magazine: all of it's important. Take the Letters column of a recent publication, for example, which contained a photograph of Miss Julie Gibson, the celebrated Philadelphia *stripteuse,* and a scolding letter from her manager pointing out that Sean O'Faolain's article on Philadelphia mentioned the Liberty Bell, but unaccountably omitted any reference to Julie. Many visitors, the letter hinted, work out their schedules so that they can gaze upon Miss Gibson before going to see the Liberty Bell. Now this is the sort of thing that we are set up to research properly, freeing the editors for more important work. Accordingly, we dropped around to Miss Gibson's shrine, a small night club called the Wedge, one night recently and annnounced that our purpose was to right any wrong that had inadvertently been done. Miss Gibson received us cordially in her dressing room, and we were pleasantly surprised to note that her competition with Independence Hall had not taken too much out of either of them. An attractive, buoyant brunette, she told us that she was twenty-two years of age, five feet four inches tall, and that her measurements, for the statistical-minded, are 35–21–35. Because of the cultural blind spot, Miss Gibson told us, a censoring body had forbidden her to perform her interpretive ballet, "The Dance of the Bashful Bride," but rather than brood about the poor judgment of city officials, she had promptly set about to create a new act which she felt was helping her hold her own as a tourist attraction.

"I offered to do the 'bashful bride' act for the liquor control board," she said, "but they turned me down. There was nothing wrong with the act. I came on dressed as a bride, and did a lot of posing—ballet style. Then I took off the veil, and then the jacket and dress, while the orchestra played music from 'Romeo and Juliet' by Tchaikovsky. Then I took off some other things but all the time I was doing ballet steps. This was a very beautiful dance." Miss Gibson told us that she had danced in Baltimore, Buffalo, Washington, Providence, and Mexico, but in none of those cities had she managed to become integrated so firmly in the cultural and historical life of the community as she had in Philadelphia. "I love Philadelphia," she said, "and I hope it's vice versa." We assured her it was, and promised to send all of our notes to Mr. O'Faolain, in Dublin, so he would never make that mistake again.

HARD KNOCKS NURSERY SCHOOL

A fellow in our office, just back from Las Vegas, was telling us about a nice-looking youngster of four or five, whose acquaintance he made one day beside a swimming pool there. The youngster, a native of Las Vegas, was of preschool age but he told our friend that he had already learned to count. Our friend inquired how high he could count, and, drawing a deep breath, the lad started off manfully. "One, two, three," he began, "four, five, six, seven, eight, nine, ten, jack, queen, and king!"

AND THE GREATEST OF THESE . . .

Some fellow told us recently of a household incident to which he had been an innocent but perplexed spectator, and it left us with the uneasy feeling that our responses to charity drives are becoming little more than reflexes. Our friend had called a Venetian blind repair man to come pick up a faulty blind, and the next morning, while the family was seated at the breakfast table, the doorbell rang. Our friend's wife went to the door, and the man outside said, "I'm here for the Venetian blind." Excusing herself in a preoccupied way, the wife went to the kitchen, fished a dollar from the food money, pressed it into the repair man's hand, then gently closed the door and returned to the table. "Somebody collecting," she explained, pouring the coffee.

ROMANCE WITH THE WEST (CONT'D.)

The candid, straightforward manner of the West always exhilarates us. Where else could you find a news story handled in such forthright way as the following item from the Monterey, California, *Peninsula Herald:*

"Miss Roberta Ford was injured while driving a car near

this city yesterday. The area in which Miss Ford was injured is spectacularly scenic."

GROUP NON-HEALTH

We've just heard of a new service that's going to be offered to hypochondriacs everywhere by an enterprising New York doctor. Each month the patients who pay the prescribed fee will receive the symptoms of a new disease, under a group plan to be known as Disease-of-the-Month Club.

WELL, ISN'T IT?

A fellow we know overheard his nine-year-old daughter talking to her girl friend, who had had the good fortune of seeing *My Fair Lady*—baby-sitting rates being what they are. It may come as a surprise to you to know that even at this age, girls aren't above a little theatrical name-dropping and the girl who had seen the show couldn't resist the temptation of telling her friend all about it. "The show," she said, "has lots of songs in it, and it's about this girl who isn't very clean and who has to take remedial reading. . . ."

LITERARY TEA

When a telegram arrived recently from Mr. Jan Mitchell, owner of Luchow's, bidding us to join him and some other *bon vivants* in honoring Ted Patrick and Silas Spitzer on the occasion of publication of their new book, *Great Restaurants of America* of which Luchow's is one, and promising considerable food and drink, we promptly accepted—mindful, as always, of our responsibility to our readers. The party was in the Lillian Russell Room of the celebrated Fourteenth Street eating place, and when we arrived both *that* room as well as the adjoining one were packed with celebrants, some of whom, we noted instantly, were carrying glasses in their hands. We were received by a young man from Lippincott's, publishers of the Patrick-Spitzer opus, who propelled us in the general direction of the bar. "There's a wonderful buffet in the other room," he said, "if you can manage to get in there." We caught a glimpse of the guests of honor backed against the wall by a photographer—a position that neither seemed to regard with a great deal of relish. Patrick gazed grimly into the camera, while Spitzer wore the expression of a moose that had somehow been betrayed by a mechanical mating call. The bulb flashed, and we moved into the next room.

The buffet table was all that it was said to be—a vast display of food arranged around roast suckling pigs and glazed turkeys—and business was unusually brisk at the adjoining bar. We recognized Eddie Condon, the jazz guitarist, who introduced us to a young man whom he identified as Johnny Windhurst, a trumpet player of some stature in jazz circles, and before we could acknowledge the introduction, a large lady joined the group and began to describe a luncheon she had attended at which a number of different brands of champagne had been served. "There was Moet et Chandon," she said, "Krug, Tattinger, Mumm's, Bollinger, Dom Perignon. . . ."

"You ought to be ashamed of yourself," Condon said. "Using language like that at a nice party."

Before this matter could be settled, Ed and Pegeen Fitzgerald joined the group, the former wearing a full set of Edwardian whiskers. "Before anyone says anything," said Mrs. Fitzgerald, an attractive blonde woman, "let me explain that Ed is growing whiskers for a part in a play." Fitzgerald smiled. "The only trouble with them," he said, "is that right at this stage the beard itches badly."

We moved away from the bar and found our progress blocked by a dark-haired man of medium build and an attractive blonde girl. "My name is Gruber and this is my wife," he said, offering his hand. "I run the London Chop House in Detroit. I also have the Caucus Club across the street. The London Chop House was listed in Mr. Patrick's book and I came all the way from Detroit to this party." We were marveling over this when a man at our elbow spoke up. "I came from New Orleans," he said. "That's even more of a trip." We all turned to him and he introduced himself as E. Lysle Aschaffenburg, managing director of the Pontchartrain Hotel of 2031 St. Charles Avenue, New Orleans. "I flew up in a Delta 880. There was nothing to it."

During the next few minutes we shook hands with Bert Bacharach, the *Journal-American* columnist, who was engaged in a search for his wife; Jerry Berns, of "21"; Al Bester, the *Holiday* writer; Hal Boyle; Ronald Searle, the British cartoonist; Ralph Hench, the advertising director of *Holiday,* and his wife; Clifton Fadiman; Ludwig Bemelmans; Al Hirschfeld; and Mrs. Ted Patrick, who promptly presented us to Mr. Herb McCarthy who was identified as the owner of Bowden Square, of Southampton. Mr. McCarthy, in turn, presented his son, and we all shook hands. While we were surveying the jostling mass in front of the bar, a large man with an amiable expression approached us and extended his hand. We recognized Tony Gugnoni, proprietor of San Marino, a midtown eating place which the Patrick-Spitzer book unequivocally declares is "certainly the best Italian restaurant in the United States." "I've moved one block east," Tony told us. "Now I have a little more room. Fourteen more tables."

"Are you still on Fifty-third Street?" we asked. He nodded. "Still on Fifty-third," he said. "But one block east of the old location."

Ted Kavanaugh, *Holiday* publicist, edged his way through the crowd escorting a small blonde girl whose face could be classified only as exquisite. Again recalling our duty to our readers, we planted ourself in their path. "This is Mrs. Jan Mitchell, the wife of our host," he said. We expressed our pleasure at the chance encounter, and she smiled radiantly. "Are you Scandinavian?" we asked. "No," she replied, smiling prettily. "English." In another moment she was gone from our life, and we took up our place in the buffet line. The inner man needs nourishment too, we reasoned.

. . . *THEN A LOCK STEP*
OFF TO THE WINGS

For a long time now, Philadelphia has been the punch line of a vaudeville gag—a sort of Pocatello or Keokuk, where the more advanced routines had to be laid away and the Golden Bantam brought out. "Philadelphia is the only graveyard I've ever seen," says Bob Hope, *"with lights."* "I'm going to Philadelphia," says a comedian from Altoona, "for a rest." And in another bit, the straight man asks, "Is your brother in Philadelphia?" and the comedian replies, "No. My brother is still living."

A few weeks after the excitement in Monaco, when Prince Rainier married the American girl whose name escapes us for the moment, a new story leaped to life. It concerned the Philadelphia family at Monte Carlo who, encountering snails on the menu for the first time, couldn't get their fill of them. Finally, the waiter asked gently if there were not snails in Philadelphia. "Yes," replied one of the gentlemen, "but somehow we never manage to catch them."

As Philadelphians, by circumstance rather than by birth, we have been reflecting on the magnitude of the injustice of imposing this jackanapes character upon our city, and we now propose to demonstrate that this character is not in accord with the facts. Falling into our hands the other day, as timely as the unexpected collection of an old debt the week before Christmas, was a modest bulletin published by the Philadelphia Transportation Company and offered as reading matter to bored riders of the subways and streetcars. The issue we examined had devoted one entire page to a listing of events that were to occur that week in Philadelphia, and it is to this that we are now pointing as proof that the man who doesn't find excitement in this town, just isn't trying. The list:

All-Parakeet Show of the Eastern Pennsylvania Budgerigar Society, Penn-Sheraton Hotel.

Penn State Cat Club annual show, Knights of Columbus Hall.

Annual Scottish Concert, auspices Scottish Clans and Daughters of Scotia, Broadwood Hotel.

The Big Eighteen Merchants Association Parade, between Lehigh Avenue and Clearfield Street.

The Annual Bazaar and Oyster Supper of the Methodist Home, Belmont and Monument Avenues.

All right, New York. Take all of the time you need for an answer.

LYSISTRATA, 20TH CENTURY A. D.

For those of our readers who were born during the past week, we would like to state that we have no fondness for cats. Just why we keep reverting to this subject, like a drunkard to his jug, has long puzzled us, but now, after considerable probing, we think we can bring out of the dark depths of our subconscious the reason for this preoccupation. We don't hate cats; what we really hate is women. Cats just remind us of women.

Sit down, fellows, we have a little lecture for you that will probably be as welcome as a coal bill in the Christmas mail. Are you willing to face the fact that in this country man has lost the dominant role for which, in the opinion of many anthropologists, he was fitted by nature? That he is so thoroughly controlled by women that the latter have dropped their subtlety and pretense, and now manipulate him in an open and shameful way? That no brainwashing has ever been devised that has been as effective as the mental detergents used by the Master Sex to convince men that they are knaves, or fools, or both? These questions come from a man who has 20–20 hindsight, but whose frontal vision requires a squint.

If the American male has lost what the Europeans call *la douceur de vivre* he need look no further than the glass from which he has been drinking to discover the source of his bitter taste. The investment houses, quite aware of the fact that women control men's wealth, now aim their advertisements—with tragic accuracy—toward the female investor. (Women shareholders own a majority of the stock.) Professional writers, with an eye to commerce, grind out an endless chain of romantic novels. (How many men take books from the drugstore's circulating library?) Tolerant of men's tastes but not the least concerned by them, women no longer dress for men but rather to impress other women. (You'd rather that your wife had long hair, wouldn't you?) Women say "my car," "my home" and "my children." (Men, for some reason, cling with pathetic futility to that old pronoun "our.") A gathering of women is an occasion of moral uplift. (A gathering of men is referred to as a "stag meeting," and is evil from the word go.) Sports in which women participate, such as golf and tennis, are "refined." (All-male sports, such as pool, are "coarse.") In the recent *roman à clef* in Monaco, space in American newspapers devoted to Grace Kelly outweighed that given her fiancé, ten tons to one. (Does anyone recall reading what the prince wore at the wedding?) A Smoky Mountain schoolboy can tell you the name of our first ambassadress to Italy. (But what was the name of our ambassador to Spain, or France, or Pakistan, or Portugal?) The newsstands are blanketed with women's magazines. (How many—successful—men's publications are there?) Attendance at ball parks is falling off in almost direct ratio to the increase in theater business. (Had your wife rather see the Dodgers than Rex Harrison?) Humor writing is fast disappearing as a literary form in America. (Women have no humor in their emotional economy, so why publish books which the buying public won't buy?) Television screens are alive with what is known in the trade as "situation comedies" but which are a succession of episodes in which the father, or husband, becomes hopelessly entoiled in a situation that wouldn't confound a third-grader, and is rescued from final catastrophe by his wife in the last few minutes before the commercial. And there is "Mutt and Jeff," and "Bringing Up Father," but so far as we know there are no comic strips or television dramas dedicated to the glorification of the triumphant male.

The argument of women, of course, is that the male is content with his downgrading. Maybe so, maybe so. But what's one man's meat is another man's high blood pressure.

WE'RE STANDING THERE, MINDING OUR OWN BUSINESS

As everybody knows we do our best to keep away from controversial subjects. Even the close observer of our work, the scholar who looks between the lines for some hidden meaning, finds nothing that will contribute to the discord of the world or create new dissension. The irritants which, on bad days, we are tempted to introduce into the public main stream, invariably turn out to be philosophical placebo. So we were amazed a few weeks ago to find ourselves flooded with mail in reply to a factual, noncontroversial little essay we had written in which we pointed out that the American woman has seized control of the country, her family, and most important—her husband. We would like to add that the essay pointed to several other previously established facts, including the assertion that the American woman had brought about her own destruction by bleaching the male to such an extent that even she found him no longer interesting. All perfectly true, of course.

Well. The response was frightening, and we are going to offer a few selected samples here to illustrate how a demonstrable truth can be brought under violent attack.

"Dear Sir:
There is no doubt about it, you are crazy.
Yours truly,
(Mrs.) V.T.G."

"Dear Sir:
"I'm a woman and I love men. I don't own any stock, as you said women did. I don't read romances from the drugstore library. If there's a man around to notice what I'm wearing, God knows I'll dress for him. I have long hair. This whole thing is man's own damn fault and we women are just waiting for him to shape up.
Best wishes,
(Mrs.) C. F."

Note to Mrs. C. F. You sound okay. If you'd care to discuss this further, you can reach me at MU 7–5300.

"Dear Sir:
  Ha!
            (Mrs.) C. P."

"Dear Sir:
  I join you in hating cats, but you shouldn't hate *good* women.

                              Sincerely
                              (Mrs.) V. H."

"Dear Sir:
  You shouldn't say women don't have a sense of humor. My publisher tells me that over a quarter million copies of my new quarter murder mystery are rapidly being snatched by women as well as men.

                              Best wishes
                              S. S. B."

Normally we'd close on that one, but there was one other letter which, while a little hard to categorize, seemed to come from a man honestly seeking to express a thought.

"Dear Sir:
  I agree with you, and I would like to add that it is not true (as women contend) that married men live longer than single men. It just *seems* longer.

                              Sincerely yours,
                              S. S. W."

A NIGHT TO REMEMBER,
OR, I'LL TRY TOMORROW

A few weeks ago we started brooding about a bygone era in volunteer fire fighting, an era that we are concerned may shortly be lost to this and succeeding generations unless steps are taken by some of us elders to capture it in ballad or drama or narrative. To dissipate our own *angst* on this score, we have whipped up the following drama which we are offering to schools and amateur groups on a royalty-free basis. Motion-picture rights can be purchased, but it's only fair to warn the film companies that the price is understandably high.

SCENE: *the headquarters of a volunteer fire company. The men appear to have just returned from a fire; they still have on their slickers and fire hats. They are sitting around uneasily, obviously getting a dressing-down from the Chief who stands facing them in front of the room. At curtain, the Chief is gazing about the room in silent contempt.*

CHIEF: Well, all I can say is another fire like that and we may as well disband. I don't think the fire was even given a chance.

WILSON (*in a conciliatory tone*): Golly, Chief, sometimes a fire will just die out of its own accord, in spite—

CHIEF (*brusquely*): This one didn't. Some smart fireman put it out. And we hadn't even got to the dining room yet.

SIMPSON (*dreamily*): Did you see that china closet in the dining room? Packed with dishes?

CHIEF: Sure I saw it. And if I went back there again I'd still see it. Not a dish was broken.

(*The men cringe at this, and flush guiltily.*)

WILSON: Curly did a good job on the piano in the living room. You got to give him credit for that—

CHIEF: Not according to my standards he didn't. (*Points finger at Curly*) Did you wet the felt? Did you wet the music rack so the sheets would stick together? Did you jam the pedals?

CURLY (*defensively*): Gee, Chief, I only got two hands.

CHIEF: Who was supposed to be working with you on the piano? One man is supposed to hold up the top while the other man hoses the felt.

SIMPSON: I was assigned to the piano, Chief, but when I saw the fire wasn't going to last long I thought I better start wetting down the books. He had a lot of books and—if I do say so myself—I got a little water on every one of them.

CHIEF (*rubbing hands*): Well, I didn't know that.

POMEROY (*eagerly*): And don't overlook my work on the radio—always get inside and crush the works first. Then—

CHIEF: That's something I want to talk to you about, Pomeroy. You're new in the company and I should have told you this before. *Never* go to work on the outside of a radio—always get inside and crush the works first. Then—if you have time—you can attend to the cabinet. Got that?

POMEROY: Check, Chief.

CHIEF: Well, that's about all, fellows. Maybe we will learn from our mistakes. And bad as we were tonight, we didn't pull anything as raw as Company No. 3 did over in Glendale last week.

WILSON: What was that, Chief?

CHIEF: You won't believe it, but I got it from good authority that they didn't even force the door. They just opened it and walked in. (*Derisive laughter and murmurs of disbelief as The Curtain Falls.*)

LEE WAS WAITING AT THE GATE WHEN GRANT GOT HIS SECTION EIGHT

Now that the Civil War has replaced Mt. Everest as the center of literary interest, we would like to offer the contents of our files to the Civil War writers, believing, as we do, that our data will reveal some aspects of the struggle heretofore concealed. All of the material collected by us was taken from highway historical markers in the South—the by-product of a recent trip—and if, after leafing through our notes, you come to the conclusion that hominy grits are indeed an hallucinogenic compound, we can only say that the decision is your own.

Among the historical markers which we feel somehow should be integrated into the general body of knowledge available on the Civil War are the following:

CONFEDERATES OUTSMART FEDERAL TROOPS; GIVE UP GETTYSBURG

After a terrific battle which lasted three days, General Lee strategically withdrew his troops from Gettysburg. It was one of the most brilliant maneuvers of the war. Meade was so disheartened at being outsmarted that his aides had to dissuade him from joining the Confederate Army, which was fighting to preserve the Union.

BIRTHPLACE OF STEPHENS

A little to the east of this sign lies the birthplace of Alexander H. Stephens, Vice-President of the Confederate States of America, who, next to George Washington and Jefferson Davis, is perhaps the nation's best-loved and most famous statesman.

INCIDENT AT VICKSBURG

While pursuing Grant's tattered Federal Army outside Vicksburg, the Confederate columns withdrew to the side of the road to permit the carriage of a young Southern girl to pass. "Thank you, Gen'l Johnston, sugah," the girl said as she passed the Confederate chieftain. The incident was typical of the conduct of the Confederate Army, which was fighting to preserve the Union.

AMBUSH AT CARTER'S GROVE

One hundred yards east of this spot, eighteen Federal infantrymen lay in ambush for a lone Confederate ranger delivering a message to General Jackson. The graves of the Federal soldiers lie to the east of Carter's Grove.

SURRENDER AT APPOMATTOX

The Northern Armies reeled backwards toward Appomattox where, on April 9, 1865, General Lee, exhausted by the fruitless chase, surrendered his sword to General Grant. "Here," he is quoted as saying, "you need this more than I do." This ended the efforts of the Confederate Army to preserve the Union.

Frankly, we had always thought that the North had put up a little better fight than it did.

NO SNOW, NO RAIN, BUT PLENTY OF GLOOM

City people don't get to the post office often, and to be perfectly frank they aren't missing much. During this past election campaign, we tried to get our local candidates off subversion and foreign policy long enough to find out what they would do, if elected, to pep up the post office lobby, but we didn't get far. It's the reading matter on the bulletin boards that bothers us. Like a lot of other country people, when we go to town to shop we usually rendezvous with our family at the post office, which means that we do an awful lot of waiting there. Or a lot of awful waiting. We can recite the Migratory Game Fowl announcement from memory and those are our free-hand drawings of canvasback ducks which you see on the old War Bond poster. We did them with a pen which was either a late Calvin Coolidge or an early Herbert Hoover, we aren't sure which. Even the post office people regard us as something of an authority on the airmail rate to the Canal Zone, Ecuador, Paraguay, Colombia, Honduras, and Central America. We don't know what to suggest but something ought to be done. If it weren't warm there, we'd wait somewhere else, that's how deeply we feel about it.

A FEW NOTES ON THE SUBJECT OF ARIDITY

A controversy over how best to make the Martini, it seems, is destined to go on and on. One group, highly articulate, argues that the volume of vermouth should be slight; another group, led by Bernard DeVoto, a Pulitzer

Prize-winning historian, and a persuasive man, holds that the proper proportion of gin to vermouth should be about pi (3.1416) to one. Another group argues that the Martini shouldn't be made *at all,* and a good case can certainly be made to support this contention. What again drew our attention to the subject, however, was the official entry of the United States Government into the controversy, and the feeling that if the Martini is to become a political issue we had better arm ourselves with the facts.

Reports from Washington leave some doubts as to how firmly the Government has committed itself in the matter, but a statement from the Internal Revenue Service pretty clearly demonstrates that the Government intends to give the subject a shake—if we may be forgiven a pun. In a recent ruling, the IRS amended its tax regulation which required bottled Martinis to be mixed with not less than one part vermouth for every three parts of the other principal ingredient, and directed that in the future the proportion may be one to five. However—and here we sense the finality of Federal authority—no more than five.

We don't intend to probe the Government's right to meddle with the thirst of its citizens, but on the contrary, we are asking for a strong united stand behind the Internal Revenue Service. Think how much better this has been handled than if the matter were thrashed out by a congressional committee. In our mind's eye, we can see the prosecutor making a strong vermouth man squirm unhappily in his chair; or the committee chairman peering innocently under his eyebrows, lulling a seven-to-one man into a false sense of security. No, it's been handled right, and we should support the ruling without regard to party. *Political* party, that is.

SICK, SICK

A friend of ours, a member of the station-wagon set, sent along to us recently a name he saw emblazoned on the mailbox of a small farm, and we wish to advise those suburbanites who have not yet named their places to forget the whole thing. It's all been said. The name our friend saw was "Psychottage."

SICK, SICK (CONT'D)

Some people can't stand to see a story go untopped. A chap from New York told us that there was a cottage similarly named near his place on Fire Island. Moreover, he said, behind the cottage was a small roadway, no bigger than a path, which bore the sign "Psycho-Path."

7

Abroad

O H

A lady we know who spent some time in Egypt this summer was telling us of a bazaar she visited in one of the side streets of Cairo. As a special attraction, she said, the proprietor was exhibiting at one end of the room "The Skull of Cleopatra." Beside it, however, was a smaller skull, and this one piqued our friend's curiosity. Rather timidly, she asked the proprietor whose skull that was. "That is Cleopatra's too," he explained kindly, *"as a child."*

THE OLD WORLD AND THE NEW

We've just had a wonderful dinner by candlelight in a fourteenth-century Tyrolean castle ("The first meal served here in four hundred years," we were told by a waiter in a Renaissance costume) and we've just sped from Milan to New York on a jet in a matter of a few hours, and the whole thing has left us with a sense of weightlessness, as though we've touched G at the tilt-over of a power climb. Beyond our window, as we write this, the grass in Independence Square is beginning to take on the sparkle of spring and on warm days, such as this, the base of the Barry statue is crowded with visitors reloading cameras and examining light meters. It's all familiar but in an unfamiliar way. Time and space control man, not vice versa, and the sooner we all learn this the less confused we will be.

Our travels, which came about as the result of thoughtfulness on the part of the Italian State Tourist Office, Alitalia, and the Province of Bolzano—the latter embracing that tiny region of Dolomite peaks and valleys just south of the Brenner Pass—were really more pleasure than business, but that pretty much describes all of our journeys. Other writers, we have noticed, keep a notebook handy, snap their cameras constantly, and are forever asking local burgomasters how to spell their last names. Now turn for a moment to us. We peer from plane windows, engage in conversation with the lady at the next table of the sidewalk *café,* wander for hours on side streets, and come home with a trifling assortment of lire, francs, and pesetas in our pockets and the guilty realization that we forgot to write post cards.

But although our notebook is unspoiled, we will remember for some time the view of Geneva from a jet plane, with Lausanne and Montreux shining in the sunlight on the other shores of Lac Léman and Mont Blanc and the Jungfrau reaching up, in blinding white, toward the plane. Nor are we likely to forget the glitter of La Scala, or the dignity of a reception held for us in the Crespi Palace of Milan by the daughter of Puccini, where, in a small drawing room late in the evening, our eighty-year-old hostess sat under a painting by Botticelli and, in perfect English, told us gravely that "No one knows how much work is involved in living in a palace." We stood early one morning in the refectory of the monastery of Santa Maria delle Grazie and gazed at da Vinci's *The Last Supper,* which is now fading and flaking from centuries of dampness and abuse, and a few hours later in Verona we sipped cappucino at a table in the Piazza Bra and watched the young girls (Capulets, all of them) flirt with their male pursuers (Montagues beyond doubt) as they marched to church on one of the first Sundays of the soft Italian spring.

We learned that the area around Bolzano is known variously as the Dolomiti, the Sudtirol, and the Alto Adige, but any of them describe a mountain-locked land that must surely contain some of the finest ski slopes in the world, as well as some of the merriest people. At Ortisei we boarded a cable car that took us, in a blinding snowstorm, to the peak of a mountain where we were met by an Alpine band and horse-drawn sleighs and whisked off to a chalet for lunch. From another cable car, a few days later, we saw the village of Merano and the hillside villa of Ezra Pound, while later we experienced the need, at a castle on the Lake Caldaro, of sampling eight choice wines, the product of the surrounding vineyards. Travel *is* stimulating.

THE WOMEN

$E = mC^2$, as Albert Einstein was fond of saying, and we wholeheartedly concur. We only wish that the intellectual and emotional structure of the female could be so crisply stated, and we say that because we have just visited two attractive and intelligent ladies, and we came away with vague misgivings about them both—misgivings which grew from the fact that they were both so forthright that naturally we have assumed they were concealing something. The first lady—in the order of our visits—was Madame Ginette Spanier, the *directrice* of the house of Balmain in Paris, who was in the United States for a few weeks to appear on some television shows calling attention to her book, *It Isn't All Mink* (Random House). "Do you want to know what *chic* is?" Madame Spanier asked, and we nodded affirmatively. "It's a mysterious star quality that is sent from heaven and that cannot be acquired. A *chic* woman can come into a room wearing a rabbit jacket, and you will think she's covered in mink from head to toe. If you ask me who has *chic*, the two people who leap instantly to mind are Marlene Dietrich and

Lena Horne. Are American girls *chic?* No, they are a little bit too overdressed to be truly *chic.* I find American girls dressing at ten o'clock in the morning the way a well-dressed French girl would dress at six in the evening."

The other lady with whom we talked was Miss Rona Jaffe, whose two novels, *The Best of Everything* and *Away From Home* (Simon & Schuster), helped establish for her the reputation of being the *enfant terrible* of contemporary American literature or the official United States answer to Françoise Sagan. An attractive wraith of a girl (ninety-five pounds) with intense, brooding eyes and a somewhat sassy manner, Miss Jaffe went to Rio de Janeiro for six weeks, liked it, rented an apartment for three months, and on the basis of her observations wrote *Away From Home.* "There were no young people there," she said, "but there was quite a colony of young married people, and the more I watched them the more convinced I became that they would make a novel. They were dull and I had a low opinion of them. The wives were bored to death with their husbands, but they went to bed with them and they went to the supermarket, so the marriages were considered good. In other words, they slept with their husbands, but they didn't speak to them. They were all terribly faithful, but it was hard to understand why." Miss Jaffe seemed completely disinterested in the fact that *Time* magazine had labeled her novels "non-books," and said she had another novel in mind but would wait two years before writing it. "A writer shouldn't write a book every year," she said, "because you burn up faster than you can replace it. Meanwhile, I'm writing a juvenile book and a musical comedy."

We asked Miss Jaffe if she had achieved her full growth. "What kind of question is that?" she asked tartly. "I achieved my full growth when I was twelve."

SEX, RELIGION, AND ROYALTY

Magnum may mean a two-quart measure of champagne to most readers, but to editors it stands for something

vastly different. To them, and to other editors throughout
the world, Magnum is the abbreviation for Magnum Photos,
an international co-operative picture agency with headquarters in New York and Paris, from which assignments
go to some of the greatest photographers and photo-journal-
ists on earth. Three of these assignments brought death to
three illustrious photographers: Robert Capa was killed in
Indochina, Werner Bischof in Peru, and David "Chim"
Seymour died at Suez. But Magnum photographers roam the
world as restlessly as ever, and their pictures have enlivened
thousands of published pages in the twelve years of the
agency's existence.

A short time ago, in Paris, we dropped around to Magnum's European headquarters at 125 rue Faubourg St.
Honoré to have a talk with Barbara Miller, an associate
editor of the outfit. Miss Miller, a slender, blue-eyed American girl, suggested we descend to a sidewalk *café* where, she
implied, conversations of this type normally take place.
"Magnum does everything in its own way," Miss Miller told
us after we had selected a table and caught a waiter's eye.
"By that, I mean it's a difficult organization to describe. We
have the greatest photographers in the world, and we have to
back them up with certain supporting services. For example,
Magnum provides documentary captions where requested,
and this involves considerable research. Also we have to help
the photographers get briefed, so to speak, before they leave
on assignments. This means getting them certain books, information on the country they are to visit, sometimes suggesting subjects. This varies from very little to very much.
It's interesting, too, the way various photographers work.
Ernst Haas, for example, looks for the spectacular panorama,
while Henri Cartier-Bresson tries to capture flavor. He likes
to linger a long time in a place and soak up the countryside.
Brian Brake has a wonderful eye for color, while Burt Glinn
is usually preoccupied with the journalistic approach. They
are all highly individualistic, and that, of course, is one of
Magnum's assets."

The waiter placed a drink in front of Miss Miller, and she

studied it before continuing. "As you would assume," she went on, "we have an enormous library of pictures, and of course our men are constantly taking new ones. These are widely sold to European magazines. This week's issue of *Paris Match* is ninety per cent Magnum. We send out everything, captions and cables, in English. Did you ever read a caption in French? You can't tell what happened."

We asked if she could tell us something about the photographic tastes of European magazines, and she laughed. "I certainly can," she said. "There are several 'golden' subjects so far as we are concerned. The Pope is one and royalty is another. Princess Margaret Rose is foolproof. Movie stars are good, regardless of what they are doing. The ideal formula is part religion, part sex. This strange dichotomy appeals particularly to the French, although it's true for other European editors as well. Then when you can add royalty—it's irresistible. Princess Grace of Monaco has it all. She's religious, sexy, a movie star, *and* royalty. Is it any wonder that she's in the European picture magazines every week?"

EUROPE REVISITED

Portofino, Italy

If there has been any demand for our notes on how Americans are deporting themselves abroad this year it hasn't been raised above a whisper, but that has not deflected us in the past from setting out—in an impartial and coldly impersonal way—our observations, and this seems as pleasant a place as any to assemble our thoughts. In the first place, let us emphasize that this is no *aria da capo* of *The Ugly American* nor is it any attempt to tidy up a muddle our fellow countrymen may have created. We intend to ask more questions than we answer.

The first question is on a point of order. Is it ethical to walk through a carefully composed photograph just as the photographer—unaware of your approach—snaps the shutter? We contend it is not only ethical but downright necessary if you are going to move around Europe at all. We tried holding back (we were all young once) when we first arrived in

Paris, but our movement through the streets of the city was so erratic that we finally took to our room and went out only after our light meter showed it was too shadowy for picture taking. Then one day as we were cutting across the Place de l'Opéra—in a hurry to get to American Express—we walked through a picture of a family posed against a backdrop of the Opéra. As nearly as we could tell, since we were walking rapidly, the father got an excellent portrait of our profile (a grim smile about the lips) with perhaps fragments of his family exposed in the background. Then, once the ice was broken, there was no restraining us. In the space of less than a block we became the central figure in fourteen other pictures, even slowing our pace down to accommodate the 1/50-of-a-second shutter speed for which we noticed most of the cameras were set. It was only when we found ourself *crossing the street* to get into pictures that we realized the thing had got the upper hand of us. Anyway, between Paris, Rome, Portofino, and Cannes, it's a safe bet that we will appear on more screens in the United States this winter than either John Wayne or William Holden.

The next subject we would like to take up is that of the youth-hostel tourists, if that is the name for the dusty, exhausted poor devils struggling under rucksacks with the pay load of a delivery truck that one sees moving across Europe like an army going into battle positions. The chief difference, however, if we may shatter our own metaphor, is that soldiers moving into combat are likely to look happier and a good deal more relaxed than the members of this army. In addition to the rucksack, every man in the youth-hostel group has a beard, the length of which indicates the point at which he ran out of razor blades. In many cases there is authority for the belief that they ran out of soap at approximately the same time. One fiercely hot day in August in Rome's central railroad station, we fell into step with an American youth who was staggering under a rucksack that, from its shape, appeared to contain not only all of his clothes but a shelf of books as well. "How's it going?" we asked. He was breathing deeply and his face was pearled with perspiration. "Wonderful," he replied, removing his teeth from his lips long enough to manage a smile, "simply terrific. Europe kills me." It seemed a distinct possibility.

We would next like to say a word about clothes, since we've noticed—or think we do—a subtle difference in the manner of dress which has occurred since last summer. Men on the French and Italian Rivieras are sticking to their tight trousers and V-neck sweaters, but this year they are wearing the sweaters tossed over their backs with the sleeves knotted across the chest. Only once have we noticed a man actually wearing his sweater, and he stood out like a student in plus fours on the campus at Princeton. The most noticeable change in women's wear is a further tightening of slacks and shorts. (Don't tell us it's impossible; we thought so too.) Perhaps some advance—we almost said breakthrough—has been made by the textile industry in the production of high-stress fabrics.

The last we want to discuss is the newest unit of the summer European social structure—that group which is bound together by the invisible ties of the Eurailpass. These people have paid $125 for the unlimited use over a two-month period of Europe's combined railroad system and—to an individual—they are dedicated to getting their money's worth. They can talk about the roadbeds of obscure branch lines with more authority than the section foremen, and they are far more familiar with the railroad stations of Paris and Florence than with the Uffizi Gallery or the Louvre. One chap we met in Rome made it a practice to take a late train to Naples every night, returning every morning. "Saves a hotel bill," he explained. We asked if he liked Naples and he shook his head. "Never been out of the station," he said. "What's it like?"

SPUTNIK-SCHMUTNIK, HOW'S THE FOX-GLOVE?

Edinburgh, Scotland

A few days ago, while enveloping a bottle of malt Scotch whisky in an old copy of *The London Sunday Times*

to cushion it from other articles in our suitcase, our eye was
caught by a headline giving a last-minute bulletin on the
strawberry situation. "A Longer Life for the Strawberry,"
the flash was headed, and it carried the by-line of Peter
Collins, the *Times's* well-known strawberry correspondent.
For some time now, we had been reading the overseas editions of the New York newspapers, and while we were well
abreast of the election news, the launching of missiles, and
the bombing of synagogues, we were lagging badly on the
strawberry situation. We read the news story, which, frankly,
left us disappointed. Strawberries suffer more than most
fruits from a very short self-life, the article declared, and an
extension of only as little as three days would make a "vital
difference." True enough, but hardly rating a scare headline.
Nevertheless, it set us wondering what else we may have
missed during the past half-year that we have been out of the
United States, so we sat the bottle down with the paper.
Skipping, for the moment, Lord Montgomery's Memoirs
(although we decided we'd come back later and read the
installment in which he criticized the strategies of General
Eisenhower, General Bradley, General Patton, General Mark
Clark, and General J. E. B. Stuart) we straightaway hit pay
dirt—a richer vein than we had topped in the New York
papers in some time. "Did you know," a *Times* editor
demanded, "that often the very same English word has two
significations quite opposite to one another?" Startled, we
read on. "This is the case with the verb *to cleave,*" the story
continued, "which means to *adhere tenaciously,* and also *to
separate by a blow.*" We had to admit he had us there, and
our only justification was that American newspapers had in-
adequately prepared us for the dive and swoop of real
journalism.

"Better By-Roads for Cyclists" was the headline of a story
that told how forthrightly Mr. Harold Watkinson, Her
Majesty's Minister of Transport, had entered the controversy
over bicycle routes. "The government has not forgotten the
man who likes to ride his cycle or moped on the by-roads,"
Mr. Watkinson declared. We aren't exactly sure what moping

on the by-roads means, but we are heartened to know that the custom has a friend in a place of authority.

The most appealing news article in the whole paper appeared on page six and was headed "Quiet Interval at Finsbury." The headline summed up the situation there nicely and left the reader free to read on, relaxed and confident in the knowledge that nothing was going on in Finsbury that required his attention. We like that; in times like these when we are almost always beyond our depth, it's reassuring to be able to let down occasionally at Finsbury and catch our breath.

The next story was the real sleeper, though. Headed "The Cow is an Addict," it carried the signature of the *Times* agricultural correspondent, Dr. F. D. Smith, and told how a cow had eaten intemperately of windfallen apples that had fermented. "She had a weak head," Dr. Smith explained in his dispatch, "and she could not hold her liquor. When milking time came in the afternoon, she rolled in dead drunk—leering at us foolishly and lurching as she came. We milked her standing up; we dared not sit under her on a milking stool. Another dairy farmer turned his thirty milking cows into his orchard and every one of them got drunk and they gave him no salable milk for over a week."

Well, the American newspapers say that if the news isn't fitten, they won't print it, but what's the matter with these stories? And, while we're asking, how about a quiet interval for New York? And see what the cows in the backroom will have.

GAETA—15 YEARS LATER

Lausanne, Switzerland

There's one chapter in the story of the last war that has never been written to our satisfaction, and that is the one dealing with the people of bombed-out villages. Where do they go? Do they ever come back? We stumbled recently, quite by accident, upon the almost totally destroyed city of Gaeta, on Italy's west coast, and we would now like to say

that we are no longer curious about this aspect of mankind's
moral digression. We had been motoring casually north from
Naples, when we came upon a long stretch of deserted Mediterranean beach. Italians, like other warm-blooded people,
go to the beach according to the calendar rather than the
thermometer, and late October, they are convinced, is no
time for swimming. We found a small hotel still open
(operated by an optimistic Italian who hoped to net an
eccentric American or two in search of a final barbecuing on
the beach) and settled down. That evening, before dark, we
drove around the point to Gaeta, hoping to find a movie or a
convivial bar. We found, instead, a pile of rubble.

It's hard to imagine what Gaeta was like before the bombs
fell, although it must have borne a similarity to other
southern Italian towns. Some of the city has been rebuilt
around the harbor, but it is quiet, ghostly, and still carries
the scent of death. There are few cars, no traffic, and the
people gaze silently from the shops clustering around the
square. A few yards up the hill begins the remains of the old
city: walls standing at dizzy angles, doors still locked to roofless buildings, arches of doorways standing crazily and alone,
the rest of the walls in rubble. It extends for blocks and
blocks, up the side of the hill. Here and there a new house
has been built from the fallen stones, but they seem strangely
out of place—as incongruous as a playground in a cemetery.
The sun caught the white plaster of one of the walls, a wall
that had enclosed a living room, and it shone as brightly as
though the destruction had occurred the preceding day. One
plaster wall contained a small round spot, where a picture or
a clock had protected the paint.

A middle-aged Italian came down the hill, picking his way
through the debris, and we stopped him. "Were you here
during the bombing?" we asked. He shook his head negatively. He had lived here, he said, but left before the bombs
fell. After the war he moved back to a house near the harbor.

"Who leveled the city?" we asked.

"The Americans," he replied quietly, "and the Germans."

"No Italian bombs were dropped?" we asked.

"No," he replied. "We provided the battleground. That's all. The bombings were all from the air, and they went on for many days. Monte Cassino is only thirty-five kilometers inland, and Anzio is not too far to the north. There was much fighting around here. Gaeta had a harbor, and it had to be destroyed." He tipped his hat and moved on down the hill, skirting the roofless walls of a four-story building.

At the top of the hill an Italian marine stood guard at a wall, in front of which was a street of toppled houses. We asked the marine what was beyond the wall, and he said it was the grounds of an Italian Naval School. We asked if the school had been there during the war and he said he didn't know. "I wasn't here during the war," he said, "and I'm glad of it."

It was getting dark as we walked back down the hill to the harbor. A small boy carrying a bottle of milk stepped out of a ruin, crossed the rock-strewn street, and disappeared into another maze of leaning walls and doorways. It was a short cut home for him, no doubt, just like an American kid would cut across a vacant lot or go through an alley.

Although the sun was shining brightly when we woke up, and the water looked green and inviting, we left Gaeta early the next morning.

ADIEU, FRANCE!

Portofino, Italy

For the present we have quit France for Italy, hoping to follow the sun. It's not too easy to crystallize impressions of a place like France so as to fix it securely in one's memory; steamy fictional stuff tends to intervene to color the account. We'd like not to forget the excitement of riding in an open-top car along the Corniche d'Or in the moonlight, the road which hangs like a shelf from the cliffside of the Mediterranean from Cannes to San Raphael. Or the neat fields and hedgerows of the Loire Valley, or the wonderful light which drew Van Gogh to Arles. All somehow touched each of the senses, not just one.

There are other memories. We can never erase from our mind the image of the French automobile driver—the most savage in the civilized world—whose primary objective is not transportation but the prevention, by terrorism, of another car's using the same highway. (We are not discussing Paris here, which is such a highly primitive society where automobiles are concerned that it must be dealt with separately.) Head-on collisions are encountered more frequently than any other kind on French highways—a tribute, if you care to call it that, to each driver's insistence on his rights.

Nor are we likely to forget the total lack of understanding of even the basic principles of traffic circulation on the part of French police. Wherever traffic is hopelessly snarled, there you will find a gendarme, blowing his whistle, waving his arms, and arguing with every driver who passes. A French policeman can be placed on a straight highway in the country, with no intersections in sight, and within five minutes he will somehow contrive to have traffic backed up in both directions as far as the eye can reach. In Menton, a small city near the Italian border, we became enmeshed in a traffic snarl that ultimately brought the movement of everything to a complete standstill. The gendarme who had achieved this masterpiece of traffic misdirection took one look at the choked intersection, mounted a bicycle, and, with a shrug of his shoulders, drove away. We finally extricated ourselves by driving across the sidewalk and through a small park, but we have the uneasy feeling that some of the cars had to be dismantled to be removed.

More than anything, though, we shall remember with admiration the French ability to discover new sources of revenue when surely it must appear that all available sources have been touched. Specifically, in this instance, we recall the one hundred-franc *couvert* added to our bill at a roadside hot dog stand where we devoured a sandwich and Coca-Cola standing. And the waterfront park in Cannes where one must pay to sit on the benches. And the railroad station where one must pay fifty francs to see a friend depart. There's a thoroughness here but it makes one think that perhaps, even now, the surface has only been scratched.

We had not been properly prepared for the Frenchman's inability to deal with new situations, and this caused considerable confusion on our part and theirs during the early days of our visit. Our chief difficulty grew out of our pronunciation of French words, and the inability of the French to understand their language unless it is spoken precisely as they speak it. Ask a Parisian where the Tour Eiffel is located, and unless you pronounce Tour Eiffel exactly as he does, he will look at you blankly and say, *"Comment?"* He can't experiment, and there's no use pushing him.

Well, France has faults. Its women are not beautiful (actually they're inordinately plain; the German and Swedish girls are the prettiest in Europe); its people do not laugh, and it has no music. But its countryside is magnificent, its wines are superb, and there's no charge—yet—to ride on the Corniche d'Or in the moonlight. Hurry.

ONE WORLD

A fellow we know dropped in to a French Consulate one warm day recently to pick up a visaed passport, and from what he saw he got the impression that he had arrived right at the height, or depth, of the mid-afternoon letdown. A leaden-eyed stenographer was typing with such a vacant stare on her face that our friend stole a glance at the paper to see what she was composing. What he saw was, "Maintenant est le temps pour tous les bon-hommes venir l'aide du parti. Maintenant est le temps. . . ."

EN SCOPE ET EN COULEURS

We have nothing but admiration for the way the French adapt American film titles to their own use. There is *l'Histoire de Benny Goodman, l'Odyssée de Charles Lindbergh, Les Frères Karamazov,* and Katharine Hepburn and Burt Lancaster in *Le Faiseur de Pluie.* But the one we like best is "God's Little Acre," currently featured as *Petit Arpent de Dieu'—l'intrigue plutôt sordide d'Erskine Caldwell.*

IDLING

We don't know whether or not French linotype operators fill out a line that's to be thrown away by writing Etaoin Shrdlu, as their American counterparts do, but a few days before leaving France we went in an office where a secretary was obviously idling at her typewriter and we bent forward to see if she was writing the French equivalent of "The quick brown fox jumped over the lazy dog's back (*Le renard brun qui court vite . . .*)." She wasn't. She was typing: *"Oui au referendum. Non au referendum. Oui au referendum. . . ."* Undecided, we thought, and we tiptoed by, careful not to disturb a friendly power while pondering its future.

ALLÔ! ALLÔ!

Cannes, France

Some years ago, perhaps fifteen, perhaps twenty, James Thurber wrote an article relating his difficulties with a French telephone. The piece was highly amusing and, as everything Thurber wrote, bore the deft touch of a man who knew what he was doing, but it was slightly anemic in its conviction. By that, we mean we were left with a suspicion that Thurber had taken a minor theme and had executed some fancy improvisation around it. But no more. After two months in a French home with a telephone, we know now that if Thurber were improvising at all, it was not in the *allegro appassionato* gait that we had suspected. In fact, we think he probably muted the whole thing.

The telephone has not yet come to France. The instruments are there, all right, and somewhere in the center of it all there is a *telephoniste* who tries (hell, we were all young once) to tie the lines together, but it doesn't work. Not only that, it doesn't even come close to working.

In the first place, and this is probably the core of the trouble, the Frenchman considers the telephone his adversary, and he lifts the receiver with approximately the same feeling of security that an alligator has in a handbag factory. He loathes it, he dials frantically and erratically, and he starts screaming the moment he gets a response. Circumstances of various kinds combine to give him the wrong number approximately eight times out of ten. Well aware of the overwhelming odds against him, he seeks instantly to place the burden of guilt on the party who responds. The other party, wounded as only the innocent can be, screams back in a compound of rage, protest, and sulk. A Frenchman whose lower lip is out is a Frenchman who has just tried to use his telephone.

During the first few weeks that we occupied our villa we tried on several occasions to use the telephone, but the results were always a good deal less than we had hoped for, so we gave up. Now the telephone rings two or three times a day, and, although we answer it with diminishing hope, it is always a wrong number. We say "Hello," the operator tells us "*Ne quittez pas*," which translates roughly into "Hold the wire," there is the sound of heavy breathing at the other end, and then the screaming starts. Once we decided to wait it out, just out of curiosity, but this bit of caprice on our part only momentarily threw the caller off balance. The screaming tapered off, there were a few seconds of silence, and, in a mild tone, the caller asked, "*Etes-vous là?*" When we indicated that we did not intend to *quittez*, his voice climbed to a new level, and the invective was resumed. It was something to hear.

One day a lady called us from Paris eighteen times, and the law of averages finally asserting itself, we were connected. The first seventeen calls, she told us, had put her in touch with several grocery stores, the Sûreté, a bakery, the Martinez Hotel, an excursion boat line, and a variety of private homes. Having spent some time in Paris, she was not the least surprised at all this but, on the contrary, expressed the view that service seemed to be improving.

Perhaps the really treacherous thing about French telephones is the fact that they *sometimes* work. Like the Sunday that our watch and clocks stopped, and we dialed the Carlton Hotel, asked the operator there what time it was, and hung up before we realized we had actually completed a call. This was the worst of all demonstrations of unreliability. At least we have the right to expect consistency.

AVEZ-VOUS VOTRE CERTIFICATS, MONSIEUR?

Cannes, France

Quite a lot has been written over the years on the subject of the fascination for the French of paper work and bureaucratic detail, but we are fresh from an encounter with a series of French organizations, official and unofficial, and form for form we'll place our experiences in competition with those of anyone. In brief, we bought a car in Paris—a car and several pounds of documents.

The car salesman was courteous and understanding, and he had knowledge of the American's failure to appreciate a well-filled form. He would see to the paper work, he explained, except the barest minimum against which he could provide no protection. We thanked him, left our passport, our Pennsylvania driver's license, Army discharge, Curtis Publishing Company building pass, a Virgin Islands driver's license which happened to be in our wallet, and a visitor's permit to enter Cuba in 1957. He was impressed by the assortment, and promised to call us within three days. The call came sooner than we anticipated—the next day, in fact. He needed our vaccination certificate, and would we care to drop by and discuss with him some details concerning our proposed membership in the Touring Club of France. Quite firmly we explained that we had no intention of joining the Touring Club of France, and quite firmly he insisted that it must be done. In desperation he placed an assistant on the telephone who, he said, could perhaps make it clear to us why the membership was required. The assistant won us over instantly: we should join, he explained, because the Touring Club of France was located on the Avenue de La Grande Armee and it had three flags flying over its door. Our membership is No. 2273326.

During the next three days, an endless stream of papers came to our hotel for signature: insurance forms, ownership forms, certificates for gasoline coupons, special insurance forms valid only for Yugoslavia (the assertion that we were not going to Yugoslavia was disregarded by everyone as utterly irrelevant), and finally the *carnet de passages en douane,* an awesome volume of twenty-five pages of certificates, each of which had been filled out in full, describing our car by *chassis,* by *moteur,* by *couleur,* and *carrosserie.* It was recorded, even, that we possessed four *pneumatiques* plus one *secours.*

Things were going perhaps too well. It was the third day, we had affixed our signature to fifty documents or more, and the end was in sight. Then came the word that there was a slight difficulty (there are no major difficulties in France) in the forms relating to our international driving license or *circulation automobile internationale.* The photographs we had submitted were not the same as those of our passport, and perhaps we would care to come by and talk things over. It was raining, but we agreed and a short time later found ourself confronting a dignified official who assured us that every effort would be made to solve the present predicament, which was slight, slight indeed. "What documents of identity do you have?" he asked. Again we emptied our pockets, adding to the earlier collection a sales slip for the trench coat we had bought in St. Louis. The official's eye lighted on the sales slip, and he reached for it. "Interesting," he said, turning it over and examining it carefully. "One doesn't often see these." We said nothing, following an instinct for self-preservation which had been greatly sharpened during the preceding seventy-two hours. Our papers and cards were scrutinized closely, a few notations were made in a volume, and the official looked up, pleased. "There should be no further trouble," he said. "Take your papers to the Touring Club, and I'm certain your *permis* will be written promptly." We gathered up our papers and started to the door. "One moment, Monsieur," the official called. "To be entirely safe, perhaps you should also take this." He held out the sales slip for the trench coat.

DEFENSE D'AFFICHER

Alfred Bester has reported in again. His communique this time deals with British library methods and suggests that while the writer may command considerable respect in America, the British have a much firmer grip on themselves in this respect. "Last week I went to the circulating library," Bester wrote, adding that he takes from Smith's on Sloane Square, "and was browsing around when suddenly I came across a copy of *The Demolished Man* by me. It gave me a funny flip, and I took the book to the desk, borrowed a pen and started to autograph the copy. The girl tried to stop me. 'It's all right,' I told her. 'I'm the author. You can charge 2d a day extra for an autographed copy.' She got mad, bawled me out for defacing Smith's property, and reported me to the manager. They're going to take the cost of the book out of my deposit."

COMPLEAT SPY-WATCHER (CONT.)

A few months ago, October to be exact, we received a letter from Eric Ambler containing an outline of an article on spy-watching. This was superior stuff and if—like us—you had been wondering about the status of the piece, we can now bring you up-to-date by means of another letter. Addressed to his agent, Mrs. Edith Haggard, of Curtis Brown, Ltd., it follows:

"Edith dear,

"I am terribly sorry not to have written you about the spy piece before this. Since I got back from the East I have been deeply involved in a movie and have only just emerged for air.

"About the spy piece; I am now going ahead with renewed confidence, but not on the bird-watching line. I shall now treat spies as big game ('With Gun and Camera in Old Stambul') and shall not limit my survey to Europe and the Middle East. The spy grounds of Indonesia, Malaya, and Thailand will also be examined.

"I shall also have far-reaching proposals for the setting up of an International Spy Reserve (to be called 'The E. Phillips Oppenheim Park') which the United States Government may care to take up with UNESCO. A provisional site for the park has already been chosen—the Ile du Levant, off the coast of Southern France. On this charming island there are plenty of disused Vauban and Napoleonic fortresses for the spies to spy on. Garrisons of disabled veterans could be provided for the spies to outwit. Escapes by boat to the mainland could be made at dead of night without risk to neighbouring shipping and in absolute safety for the spies themselves. Female spies, in traditional black satin, will, of course, be introduced for breeding purposes. Spies would be classified by vintages. It might also be possible at a later date to provide a small atomic pile for the newer types to spy on. But let us get the principle accepted first.

Love,

ERIC"

FISCAL NOTE

The current story about the cowardly counterfeiter (who has the first dollar he ever made) is singularly timely for Americans traveling in Europe this year, where some rather odd U.S. bills have been turning up. One tourist, in trying to get rid of a fifteen-dollar bill that had somehow been pressed onto him, made a dollar purchase in Paris, passed over the strange bill, and requested his change in U.S. dollars. He was amazed to get two sevens in return.

ABSINTHE MAKES THE HEART GROW FONDER

A friend of ours, just back from France, turned up quite a literary find in one of the bookstalls along the Seine in Paris. It was the French reprint of an American book and it bore the title, *Pernod and Sam* by Booth Tarkington.

8

A Feast of Reason

ANNUAL REPORT

About this time of the year, most corporations are issuing their annual reports and unless there has been a startling improvement in this form of literature since last year, stockholders across the nation are in for some dreary reading. We were pleased recently to stumble across an annual report, which struck us as a model for such documents. Clear, terse, straightforward, it breathes reassurance to the stockholder. We print it below in its entirety.

Annual Report, Bar Committee,
National Press Club

The Bar Committee is able to report an excellent year financially and socially, and the New Year picked up immediately after the "good resolutions period" (Jan. 1 to noonday) expired. The program for this year is a repeat of last: good merchandise, proper prices, the best of service. The water-wagon crowd has proved to be loud but ineffective.

The Committee has adopted a credo, supplied from the

186]

message of Prime Minister Churchill to the British Minister of Food, in wartime. We know the House Committee will subscribe to its sentiments: "On no account reduce the barley for whisky. It would be most improvident not to preserve this characteristic British element of ascendency."

RAZE LOW THE ROOF BEAM, CARPENTERS

A handsome brownstone house is being razed across the street from us, thrusting us into a conflict between two seemingly irreconcilable groups: the progress-at-any-price group, who seem determined to turn New York into a city of glass, and the stodgy holdouts, who feel that the nontransparent brownstone offered comfort, livability, and the charm of a gracious and bygone period. The cornice of a magnificent bay has just tumbled to the ground in a cloud of mortar-dust, as we write this, and the workman is gazing over the edge, as though shocked at his own vandalism. Our position is with the holdouts; we harbor a dread that the whole activity is tragically misdirected. Rachel Carson showed us how, aiming at a weevil, we exterminated the eagle; aiming to save man from malaria, we have probably given him cancer. Now, seeking to create the all-efficient, sterile, living-factory of the planners, we have probably eliminated the home.

There is some peculiar private quality to wallpaper, and one recoils slightly at the sight of it exposed on a partly demolished wall. Across the way, on what is left of a third-floor bedroom, a yellow wallpaper flecked with a small design is revealed amid the debris. It is like a lady whose slip is showing. Was it a pleasant bedroom, we wondered, and did that design, slight as it was, irritate the occupant when he was sick abed, and spent the day staring at the walls and ceiling? With no trouble at all, we can trace out to this day the design in the wallpaper of the room where, as a child, we sweated out a case of scarlet fever.

This particular brownstone was sturdily built, and we

can't help exulting in the stubborn way that it resists the wreckers. A few months ago it took three workmen, straining at their wrecking bars, to pry off the top of a window sill. A pigeon came in suddenly, without tower clearance, and was refused permission to land. After coasting over the wreckage, with eye cocked first right and then left, it glided on uptown. Everybody is fascinated by destruction.

The man in the next office, to whom we have just called, estimates the brownstone was built around 1875. (He also said, "Isn't it a shame?" which places him, too, on the side of the holdouts—as the losing group is known.) The mechanics of the home have undergone many changes since the house was built. An electric refrigerator, for example, was brought in ("It makes its own ice, right there in the kitchen") and in our mind's eye we can see the excitement that caused: those first few days when it was turned up too high with the result that the milk and eggs froze, and the owner threatened to have it removed. With a brownstone like this, the owner was certain to have been a sort of Father Day figure. By the time the oil burner replaced the coal furnace, with the coal munkers converted into laundromats, the house was accustomed to change, and most of the hight had gone out of it. But a house like this had pride, and knew that glass was a material for windows and not for walls.

An endless train of trucks is moving down Fifty-third Street now to cart away the rubble, and in a couple of days the premises will be level and ready for the new temple of crystal. We are sure it will be glistening, and soundproof, and sterile, and free of soot in the air and dust underfoot. And also, alas, free of memories, warmth, and the cry of a human infant in a nursery whose wall is covered in yellow wallpaper flecked with a small design.

THE SUMMING UP

The writer has a disarming way of suggesting by a casual shrug that he can't imagine how he got mixed up in all this. After Pogo was banned in Tokyo because a pig in one of the sequences bore a striking resemblance to Premier Khrushchev, Author Walt Kelly said, "I'm against all extremes—the extreme right, the extreme left, and the extreme middle." Upon reaching the age of eighty, P. G. Wodehouse recorded his feelings as follows: "The thought that I shall never have to wear a paper hat again is a very sustaining one." Alec Waugh, British novelist, declared, "As matrimonial timber, a novelist is the world's worst bet." This, he explained, is not because a writer has "less moral stamina" but rather because "the routine of his life is extremely hard to fit into the matrimonial pattern." A considerate man, Mr. Waugh is unmarried.

Having tried the bath water and pronounced it temperate, Sir Alan Herbert, author-humorist, took the plunge. Campaigning to have authors paid when their works are borrowed from libraries, he announced that he would make every effort to keep public libraries and the British Museum from getting copies of his next book. Speaking of libraries, the National Library Week's 1963 observance will be directed—no doubt with affectionate sincerity—by one of America's leading television broadcasters; this is the stuff that dreams, and schizophrenia, are made of. Farouk, former King of Egypt, sued Lyle Stuart, a New York publisher, for $400,000 claiming he had been libeled when a Stuart book quoted a Miami lady as saying the ex-monarch had visited her bordello in 1955. Farouk's lawyers offered a dossier from the State Department which indicated that the deposed king had not made a "state visit" to America that year. Joseph Coogan, a Philadelphia novelist, said, "For the most part, I had a happy childhood, which seemed fine at the time, but which is a great drawback to a writer trying to recall those first perceptive moments of great meaning." Louis Simpson, whose first novel, *Riverside Drive*, was published by Atheneum, said of reviews: "I won't be reading the reviews, good or bad. My opinion of book-reviewing is very low. I've seen—as anyone who reads must have—mediocrity touted in the newspapers and magazines while work with a spark of real interest was neglected. Most book-reviewing is bland, or off the point, or downright venal." *Riverside Drive* was not received by the critics with what may be called unbridled passion.

A British magazine suggested that the noun for a female dog be changed from bitch to something more "appropriate and acceptable," which indicates that the behavior patterns of animals may be moving in an opposite—and higher—direction than those of humans.

Geoffrey Bocca, author of *Bikini Beach* (McGraw-Hill), announced that one of his hobbies was bad food. "Any loon can be interested in good food," he said. "It takes a connoisseur to really appreciate horrible food." Bocca lives on the French Riviera, where one suspects there is ample opportunity to feed his whimsey.

Perhaps the yeastiness now stirring up writers is a wholesome thing for contemporary literature. With a few exceptions, their exuberance in recent years has gone from economical to spare, from spare to bony. We had cocktails one afternoon recently with a writer who had just left a meeting of the Authors Guild. "As God is my judge," he said, draining his glass, "I've seen more life at High Mass."

WHAT IS SO RARE . . .

We don't know why items like this are not widely reported in the press, because it should be obvious to even the most myopic of editors that while this represents a cloud no bigger than a man's hand it will most assuredly grow to obscure the sun. In Boston, a diner strode in indignation from a restaurant, refusing to pay his check on the ground that while he had expressed preference for his steak to be served to him rare, it had—so far as he could determine—not been placed on the fire at all. We are sorry not to have been present, because we feel it was a fateful moment in history.

Sooner or later, of course, the distinction had to be drawn between rare meat and raw meat, and it has been pretty apparent, with meat coming from the kitchen redder and redder, that the issue was building to a crisis. Nevertheless, the Boston incident displayed a degree of disunity in the gourmet cult rarely, if ever, achieved before. In this country, where all of our disagreements are more or less openly arrived at, the well-done group is sure to make the most of it, and there's not much doubt where the laughter, which you now hear, is coming from. Despite the fact that we feel the Boston diner's sense of importance collided with his sense of humor, the incident is bound to serve a purpose, if none more monumental than causing us to pause and weigh our motives. Is fashion now demanding meat to be rarer and rarer, as it demanded our Martinis to be drier and drier a few years ago?

Peter DeVries, describing a man in a white suit at a garden party whose fork penetrated a paper plate from which he was eating rare roast beef, said the guest, leaving the party, resembled nothing so much as an intern calling it a day. More recently, reports have come in of diners instructing waiters to merely hold the steak between their hands for a few moments before serving it. The restoration of body temperature to a steak is now an affront to many. Well, when one door shuts, another opens, and already those who hold the belief that the discovery of fire led the way in the long march from the jungle are beginning to speak up, and it may well be that we are about to witness a resurgence of those who fancy their meat medium to well. As in all matters of taste, our impartiality is unassailable and we call attention to the Boston incident only to tear another veil from the human mystery. The fire of controversy is lit, and for all we know it may some day sear a steak.

BACK TO ABNORMAL

We occupy a desk in one of the estuaries leading to the newspaper rack, and we notice some strange things have happened this year. Not alarming things, necessarily, but curious things. The International Air Transport Association reports that a new law now specifies that "no person shall enter or attempt to enter any aircraft in flight." We intend to abide by the regulation. A man in Tucson, eying Moscow and Washington nervously, has proposed a national essay contest, with survival space awarded as prizes, on subjects such as "Why I Deserve to Survive" and "Why I (If I Survive) Would Impeach Earl Warren (If He Survives)." An advertising agency called Creative Associates, Inc., was awarded the account of Nuclear Survival, Inc., whose product—unless it is the universal dream of mankind—remains a mystery.

In the world of art it appears that this year will be one of drama, dissension, and discord. A chimpanzee named Beauty knocked out a few abstract canvases which were sold in New York for $5,000, this strengthening the suspicions of many people about abstract art. Reports that one of Beauty's paintings—her favorite—could be found in the current Guggenheim Exhibition were described as without foundation. An expert on Picasso was stabbed by an unknown assailant in Nimes, France, and police, at last reports, were trying to determine whether the assault was only an expression of distaste for Picasso's work. Evidence pointed in this direction.

In the Dominican Republic, the capital city, Ciudad Trujillo, reverted to its historical name of Santo Domingo, and in Russia, Stalingrad became Volgograd. The minute someone starts messing around with Washington, we will advise you.

From South Africa and Alabama came two rather startling announcements on the racial question. The South African government, in a generous move, ruled that Japanese gentlemen could have honorary white status in hotels and park benches, but not in sexual intercourse. The Chinese didn't make it in any category. The State of Alabama, in what was described as a "scientific" approach to the issue, hired an anthropologist to conduct a study to "support the contention that the white race intellectually is superior to the Negro." The anthropologist is from North Carolina.

The fox-hunting controversy broke out anew in England,

where it is almost as grave as the Berlin situation. A man named Samuel Thomas shot a hunted fox and was immediately and publicly denounced by the local Master of Fox Hounds as "unsporting." Support came unexpectedly from the League Against Cruel Sports, who offered Thomas a medal for his "courageous and humane act." Thomas, who appears to be woefully lacking in the stuff from which controversial figures are cast, said he thought it was a hare. Sorry.

A report from Japan announced that Tokyo police are anticipating a bad summer so far as women being pinched by flirtatious males is concerned. Having established a direct connection between summer heat and the incidence of pinching, police findings revealed that plump girls have the most to fear and that pinchers seem to prefer girls with permanent waves. More and more, it appears, the East is becoming occident-prone.

THE CATCHER IN THE WRY

Book critics (stop us if we are wrong about this) can deal with anything but literary success. They can discover with glee a promising first novelist, shake their heads in sadness when the second effort is published with embarrassment, or bury an ancient author with a retrospective eulogy that he may have listened for in vain during his lifetime. But if an author makes the absurd mistake of achieving success—as J. D. Salinger has done—then he'd better march stoically to the woodshed and get it over with. There's no other way.

Publication of Mr. Salinger's most recent book will start an arc of brickbats moving in his direction the like of which we have never seen, largely because we have never seen anything like the peculiar success of this author. The undeniable leader of the present wave of brilliant American writing, Mr. Salinger is a craftsman so skilled that every line—and especially his dialogue—is practically poetry. Moreover, he has turned his back on sex as a subject of primary shock and amusement and works unashamedly with love and sentiment, two stray lambs he seems to be struggling to bring back to the fold. But it is Mr. Salinger's success that will outrage critics most, not the style or content of his work, and already we have an indication of the way the detractors will zero in on their target. In the August issue of *The Atlantic*, Alfred Kazin apologetically asserts, "I am sorry to have the use the word 'cute' in respect to Salinger, but there is absolutely no other word that for me so accurately typifies the self-conscious charm and prankishness of his own writing and his extraordinary cherishing of his favorite Glass characters." Thus, after bloodying the water, Mr. Kazin moves on and the other sharks can come in for the kill.

A great deal of the criticism that has been leveled at Salinger in the past seems concerned with the fact that the author's mythical Glass family seems real to many people, just as Romeo and Juliet seem real to some of us. Why this should be considered as anything more than a tribute to the author's skill escapes us, but if it has validity as criticism, we contend it is the critics who have made it so. In an article called "The Salinger Myth," in the London publication *Twentieth Century*, David Leitch broods over Holden Caulfield, the central character of Salinger's only novel, *Catcher in the Rye*. Leitch, going far beyond the text of the novel, writes, "To me it always seems that Holden comes nearer to having a sexual relationship with Phoebe than he does with anyone else." Phoebe happens to be Holden's sister, and if this bit of erotic dynamite lies submerged under the text, we can only say that we have misunderstood what appeared to us to be a very simple and moving narrative. In *The Fiction of J. D. Salinger*, a slight book (in every sense of the word) put out by the University of Pittsburgh Press, Frederick L. Gwynn and Joseph L. Blotner, say: "Salinger's career—one discovers on examination—has been a slowly maturing and then suddenly bloating process: it was bogged down in trivial magazine tales for a half-dozen years, was apparently released by the experience of World War II, came to a height with a half-dozen stories and a novel in the 1948–1951 period, and has been declining recently as its noble attempt to adapt a habitual satiric style to almost purely religious themes has become self-conscious." Well, that takes care of the rise and fall of J. D. Salinger, with the exception, of course, of a few collectors of moonbeams, such as us and the several hundred thousand other people who think he is perhaps the possessor of the greatest literary talent in the United States today.

STIR UNTIL . . .

We've watched—at first hungrily—the parade of cookbooks going by, and then gradually we lost both our interest and our appetite. As nearly as we can tell, just about every magazine in the country has published its own cookbook, with the possible exception of *Science and Mechanics* and *The London Economist*. There is one that has just appeared, however, and we are willing to call your attention to it because we feel this one should have been done. It is called *Mud Pies, and Other Recipes,* by Marjorie Winslow. Our congratulations to the publishers, Macmillan, and we hope they have a runaway best seller.

FULL VALUE

Remember the story a few years ago of the lady driver who offered a push to a stalled motorist and who backed up to get up speed and slammed into the stalled car going nearly forty miles an hour? Her explanation was that an automobile with an automatic transmission had to be going about thirty-five miles an hour before the motor would start. Well, a fellow told us a story last week that a Connecticut garageman told *him,* and it concerned an elderly lady stalled on the Merritt Parkway who had telephoned for a tow car. After agreeing on a price, the front end of the car was raised and the two vehicles proceeded on to Wilton, where the lady emerged with a satisfied glint in her eye. "Fifteen dollars seemed a little steep," she said severely, "so I decided to make you work for it. I kept the brake on all the way."

POEM WRITTEN EXACTLY FIVE MINUTES AFTER READING A MAGAZINE SUPPLEMENT ON "WRITING IN AMERICA"

We would like to say, here and now, that
    we are willing
To pass up anything written by Alfred Kazin,
    Gilbert Highet, and Lionel Trilling.
And although we've read them diligently
    we still do not know
What the hell's eating W. H. Auden,
    Archibald MacLeish and C. P. Snow;
All of whom appear to be absorbed in the
    dullest of games:
I.e., to see how many times they can
    introduce the name of Henry James.

FOOTNOTE TO LYSISTRATA

We wonder if Miss Anne Scott-James, who writes a column for a London newspaper, would be interested in an honest proposal of marriage? We address this reckless inquiry to her after reading from her column the following:

"If only I had had sense enough to stay stupid. We women are taking on a man's world—and it's hell. In fifty years' time there'll be only one sex, the way things are going. For my part you can take back our education, our jobs, our cars, our votes, our independent money. I'd trade it all in for the pleasure of being clinging, dizzy, kittenish, wide-eyed, scatterbrained, frivolous, extravagant, or just plain dumb for just one year."

This is a noble idea and we regret that it will attract so little attention. The career girls who stumble across it will smile sardonically and, gulping their vitamins and fingering

their hair to make certain it is cut short enough, mutter
something to the effect that it is the work of a female Uncle
Tom. Older women—the disabled veterans of the war between
the sexes—will speak tolerantly of the foolish things that
Spring impels poorly disciplined girls to say. And men, still
smarting from the worst defeat they have suffered since the
world began, will wonder what sort of Trojan horse is this
that has been dragged up during the night and placed among
them. But not us. We believe Miss Scott-James; we believe
she is not only an honest and sincere girl but perhaps one
who may be destined for great fame.

Albert Schweitzer said he did not believe Admiral Strauss's
press releases on the benign effect of Strontium 90 fallout,
and although he was called senile, meddlesome, and communist at the time, there is now an uneasy muttering heard
across the land when the subject of death dust is mentioned.
Miss Scott-James may be unwittingly playing such a role and
in a drama almost as grand. As the scene expands and lightens,
perhaps other women may walk on the stage and say that
there are greater tragedies than being born female. Some
may even express contentment with their femininity, or are
our lids beginning to droop as we lose touch with reality and
slip farther into the dream world?

Being a woman is a relative thing, and the feminine character, even at its most recessive, can perform wonders. Still
green in our memory is a five-week period we spent in an
Army hospital during the war, when the only woman in our
life was a battle-scarred Army nurse beside whom a lady
wrestler would appear as fragile as Elizabeth Barrett Brown-
ing. Even the patient in the next bed, an injured volunteer
paratrooper who had been a steel puddler in civilian life,
winced when she entered the room. But her hand, searching
a forehead for a trace of fever, was cool and her smile, when
she had time to be amused, was warm, and before any of us
realized it we were all locked in flirtation with her.

E. B. White says, "Man's most persistent dream is of a
forest pool and a girl coming out of it unashamed, walking
toward him with a wavy motion, childlike in her wonder, a

girl exquisitely untroubled, as quiet and accommodating and beautiful as a young green tree. That's all he really wants."

We hope that someday our grandson, if we have one, will walk through Westminster Abbey and in the Poets' Corner —because that's where it belongs—he will see a stone bearing this simple inscription:

Anne Scott-James
Woman

ONWARD AND UPWARD

Now that culture has reached down to lift to its level a number of us who, in our time, were perfectly content with the Coon-Sanders Orchestra, Vilma Banky, "Whispering Jack" Smith, and "The Plastic Age," we think a little help should be extended to some of the more stubborn cases among us who are still faltering over full acceptance of Picasso, Oistrakh, Albert Camus, and the Kabuki Dancers. It's not that we don't want to embrace the cult and be fashionable; it's just that some of the sharp edges of culture will have to be rounded off, here and there, in the interests of comfort.

Always in the forefront of any move toward self-improvement, we have worked out the following course which can convert almost anyone into a cultural snob overnight. Learn how to handle these basic situations, and you're well on your way to being not only difficult to get along with, but almost impossible.

1. At foreign movies, start to laugh a few seconds before the English subtitles are flashed on the screen. This convinces everyone, of course, that you are following the dialogue.

(a) When a mountain range, *any* mountain range, is shown on the screen, let go with a plaintive gasp, and say, "Ah, the Vosges." Don't say it to anyone in particular; rather let it *escape* from you.

2. When you enter an art gallery, walk up to a painting, study it a moment, and say, "It looks so much better now that

it's finished." This implies that you not only know the painting, but that you were in on its development.

(a) It's also impressive to gaze at a painting, pick out the
artist's first name, and say, "Luigi is still fascinated with those
Mediterranean blues." If there's any blue at all on the canvas
this is a safe comment.

3. It's easy to discuss books you haven't read, but always
keep your comments general rather than specific. An observation that never fails to bring credit to the speaker is something like this: "Faulkner's last book would have been superb
if he could only have concealed his anxiety." Or "Faulkner's
last book was weakened by his poorly concealed hostility."
Either comment can be made to fit any writer under discussion, since all writers are anxious and hostile.

(a) It is assumed, of course, that the speaker will have the
good taste to conceal or qualify his admiration for any book
written by anybody at any time. A lapse here is sufficient to
wash the student out of the culture course.

(b) Since Stendhal and Dostoevsky are currently fashionable, it is quite in order to speak fondly of a book by describing it as being in the "Genre of Stendhal or Dostoevsky."
This can be applied to any book, including *Tarzan of the
Apes,* which is truly in the genre of Dostoevsky.

4. Anything from England is better than anything from
America, because it's from England. We're sorry we can't
explain this, but that's the way it is. The Stratford (Connecticut) Shakespeare Repertory Company was pretty good,
but were you lucky enough to see the Liverpool Police
Department Dramatic Club's presentation of *King Lear?*
Ah . . . !

LOOK BACK IN ANGUISH

We've just finished reading Clifton Fadiman's "Party
of One" column in which he wonders aloud whether the
writer in America is being treated as tenderly as he deserves,
and this capped for us the pyramid of comment which seems
to have been building up—almost feverishly, at times—on the

author as the object of love. Fadiman's observations are sly
and brilliant and recognize the symbiotic relationship between author and reader, but they nonetheless suggest that
as a writer he may be squirming somewhat in a hellbroth of
his own. Earlier, we had received a printed post card from
Daniel S. Mead, a New York literary agent, which advised us
that "ALL THE WORLD LOVES AN AUTHOR!" In
smaller type, but with a full heart, Mead promised that "You
too can find love and affection, and royalty checks, through
writing." For some time now, we've been connected with the
flimsy business of writing, and we have had the good fortune
of cashing a few of those royalty checks, but we feel cheated
out of the love and affection to which we now understand we
were entitled. A few years ago Norman Cousins, the editor
of *The Saturday Review,* wrote a book bearing the curious
title, *Writing for Love or Money.* We haven't read it, but we
have read *The Living Novel,* edited by Granville Hicks
(Macmillan) and, in view of the way the chins of writers seem
to be trembling, were not surprised to find him saying
". . . serious novelists are working in a culture that is largely
unsympathetic to them."

Try as hard as we might to keep out of controversies, here
we go. In the first place, while we know a few writers who
have been pushed around like parsley, many of them have a
pretty good life and manage to put by quite a little. From our
own experience, we know that when we have finished a piece
that pleases us, we feel like a million dollars, before taxes.
The trouble is, we believe, that writers are smarting from
the lack of acclaim and public devotion which is heaped
upon movie stars and theatrical personalities; their grip on
the public imagination is shaky. Eudora Welty is a first-rate
writer but Jayne Mansfield is—we're groping for the right
word—better-loved. (Perhaps Miss Welty doesn't serve the
needs of the whole man, so to speak, but her position in the
creative firmament should be no less secure.) This isn't always
tied to physical appearance; you could pass Rock Hudson in
the Automat, where he may be working out a selection between the Danish and the apple cobbler, and not even notice

him, but the towering, rangy figure of John O'Hara or the brooding countenance of John Steinbeck would surely arrest the eye. Rather, we think the trouble with writers is that they're too accessible, too amiable. You'd stand about the same chance of getting Rita Hayworth on the telephone as you would of completing a station-to-station call to Elizabeth II. You can't even get a fashion model to answer her telephone. (There's no particular reason to drag models into this essay, other than to remark that—as a group—we don't care for them. Psychologists may even classify us as mannequin-depressive, which isn't a bad pun the first time you hear it.) But with writers, it's different; they even want to come around and loiter away the afternoon on your front porch. Now if writers have even a fraction of the perception they've led us to believe they possess, they should know the hazards of wearing their mantles too lightly. Considering what friendly, accessible fellows they are, what fan magazine would ever publish an article probing into the personal lives of, say, Bruce Catton or Sean O'Faolain? If the fan magazine editors, or anybody else, want to know what these two are up to, all they have to do is dial the number correctly. But we must warn you to start chilling a few bottles of beer, because both writers are likely to drop by in a few minutes.

NO SIDE EFFECTS?

It appears now that dalliance is far more attractive to nations than matrimony. The divorce rate has soared to the point that the few countries remaining united, such as Great Britain and the United States, are looked upon as stodgy old couples who don't know what they're missing. China has just split up with Burma on grounds of mental cruelty; the neighbors are known to be talking about Poland and Russia; Turkey and Greece are bickering over the custody of their child, Cyprus; and France is making poor progress in patching up its trouble with Algeria. Today things seem to have taken a turn for the worse: Colonel Nasser has claimed the Suez Canal for Egypt, more trouble has occurred on the border of

Israel, and, closer to home, our electric razor suddenly went dead without warning, leaving half of our chin unshaved. In Independence Square, just outside our window, there's not a single school kid in sight, despite the fact that this is the middle of the tourist season, and even the pigeons seem to be standing around uneasily, awaiting better times.

We have just come into possession of a new tranquilizing drug and we are so fascinated by the label that we find ourselves reacting to it in a way that can only be classified as a tropism. The label suggests that the drug will enable us to cope, will ameliorate our mood, and will provide us with detached serenity. You couldn't ask for more. We are watching hopefully, as we write this, for the effects of the first pill to be demonstrated, and already, we must faithfully report, the pigeons seem to be less apprehensive. Can we hope that the Chinese will apologize for failing to recognize the Burmese frontier, that the Algerians and French will get together, and that the British—coked to the gills on our tranquilizing drug—will announce plans for digging a new canal, east-west, through the middle of Africa? Meanwhile, though, we're going to play it safe and send out our razor to be fixed.

HEART

Conversation between two men overheard on Central Park South: "Honestly, this doctor is one of the sweetest guys alive. When he hears that a patient can't afford an operation, you know what he does? He touches up the X-ray plate."

HOW'S THAT AGAIN?

You know that column in most newspapers called The Inquiring Reporter which features the answers to a stock question by a group of people selected at random? The other day a Washington paper saw fit to select as its question, "What Would You Do If You Were Suddenly Made President of the National Press Club?" Among those to whom it put the question was Frank Matera, the club's bartender. Mr. Matera replied as follows: "I have seen so many presidents of the National Press Club come in and pass out, that I guess I could take the job in stride."

THE PONY EXPRESS

Things haven't changed much in schools, so far as the classics are concerned, if we can believe the story told us recently by a young man home for the spring holiday from an eastern prep school. A Latin class there, he related, was translating Cicero with the unofficial help of ponies, when the instructor startled the students by announcing that the translation would be resumed where it had left off. "That's line four on my book," he said, "and line eight on most of yours."

AND IF ELECTED,
AND I THINK I WILL BE . . .

This is the year of the big vaudeville show, with candidates resplendent in blue shirts, which absorb the glare from the spotlights, and pancake make-up, which artfully conceals both age and pallor and restores to weary politicians the ruddy vigor of a grade-B Western hero. There will be speeches, flags, music, and, for the boys in the backroom, a bottle on the shelf. Promises will be made in good faith and some in the rankest kind of hypocrisy. The din will be deafening, the television channels choked with argument, and ill will, we predict, will be in possession of the land.

To help you get your money's worth for your vote (a figure of speech; nothing more) we are offering a standard against which we ask that you check your candidate. The beauty of this standard is that it isn't scientific, and while your findings will not deliver you into a state of ataraxia they may bring your candidate into focus, perhaps even with devastating clarity. If so, good; and if you get any coins in change, strike them on the counter to check them for a hollow ring. In an election year, you can't trust anybody.

Keep your eye on the candidate who says ". . . and on the other hand" because he is arguing both sides of the question and hopes to get you going or coming. A candidate is entitled to work only one side of the street.

Be especially alert for the candidate who steps out of the parade to shake hands with the legless veteran. You are witnessing theater.

Look out for the candidate whose American Legion cap fits poorly. He just bought it.

Avoid the candidate who considers the hot lunch for school children about as controversial an issue as he cares to come to grips with.

Avoid the candidate who smiles too much. What's so damned funny?

It may be hard to do, but keep your eye on the ball when one team claims all the patriotism. Samuel Johnson said "Patriotism is the last refuge of a scoundrel," and Johnson, as you well know, was a man of rare perception.

Take a second look at the candidate whose voice falters at the end of each page of his speech. He doesn't know, any more than you do, what's coming next.

Most candidates this year are going to be Abolitionists. Check what they say in Mississippi.

When the presidential candidate bestows his blessing upon the local official running for re-election, the rules require the presidential candidate to pronounce correctly the name of his good friend.

That's it, candidates. Now who among you hears cries from his country for succor?

IT'S A DATE

We've heard a lot of Toscanini stories since the maestro died, but a writer named Pete Gorstin has come forward with one of the most amusing. Gorstin tells of Toscanini's efforts to reward a diligent chambermaid at the Hotel Astor by offering her two tickets to one of his concerts. "Tell me," he said benignly, "would you like to go to the concert Tuesday evening?"

Looking up from her dusting, she said, "Is that the only night you get off?"

IMPROVISATION

From Los Angeles, a city that we are coming more and more to regard as the cultural heart of America, comes the following advertisement of a local night club:

> 6 Dancing Girls!
> 5 Beautiful Costumes!

OH

As the close students of our work know by now, we are a pushover for the forthright statement. For that reason, we were delighted with a story told us recently by a fellow who overheard two girls talking on a crosstown streetcar. "This fellow," said one girl, "took me to his apartment and showed me a closet that contained five absolutely perfect mink coats. And guess what? He *gave* me one of them."

"What did you have to do?" asked her cynical friend.

"Just shorten the sleeves," said the first girl.

NOEL

The State of South Carolina, we have just learned from an Associated Press dispatch, is going to buy a new electric chair because the old one, installed in 1912, is "no longer considered safe." This expression of warmth and concern puts us to shame. Whether this represents the ultimate in paternalistic welfare or the ultimate in hypocrisy, we can't say, but we have a deep conviction that the story was badly underplayed by the nation's newspapers.

When a state puts one of its citizens to death but at the

same time displays anxiety that the condemned man's health may be impaired during the process, the basic dilemma of the advocates of capital punishment, it seems to us, is starkly revealed. On the one hand is the odd reasoning that the only way to guide a man into paths of righteousness is to first kill him, while on the other there is the nagging suspicion that a new crime is being committed. Once, many years ago, we were invited to a Christmas dance in a small city in Virginia where the music was to be furnished by a three-piece band, the members of which worked and were supported in their musical enterprise by a local market. The invitation—we recall it clearly—asserted that the music was to be by the Nichols Fresh-Killed-Poultry Serenaders. We didn't go.

Hearts were lifted a few weeks ago when we were told by our newspapers that American scientists were putting the finishing touches to a neutron bomb, one that would kill on a wide scale but would not destroy property. There's something uncomfortably close to South Carolina's out-of-date electric chair here, and the more we ponder it the less we like it. The implication is that property is of more value than human life. Kill all you want but don't smash the windows, or else you'll get into serious trouble. Regardless of what philosophy we have each evolved to help us live in the shadow of the bomb, we all have our fears locked within us, and we seriously doubt that we are going to be comforted very long by the knowledge that our possessions will survive us. Personally, we wish our scientists would get back to their charts and come up with a bomb that could do all the damage anyone could yearn for, but one that would still permit man to dig himself out of the rubble and go on planning future wars. The neutron bomb has done little to make a shaky future any more promising.

We have been casting about for a Christmas thought here and we think we've got it. Suppose South Carolina got rid of that old electric chair (somebody is going to get killed with that thing yet) and didn't replace it. Suppose we decide that hydrogen bombs, give or take a few hundred megatons, are about as far as we care to go right now in the direction of oblivion. Suppose we eased up on things that make people edgy. If this line of thinking appeals to you, we'd do our level best to get the Nichols combo—as soon as the turkey season is over—to drop around and beat out a few Christmas carols.

Conclusion

It is sad to tap out the ending to a book. Whether a piece has been written in anger, or despair, or jubilation, or only in haste, it remains an example of the poetic quality with which the writer invests experience. Wordsworth declared that "a poet . . . rejoices more than other men in the spirit of life that is in him," but Wordsworth should have extended this definition to include not just poets but all writers. The ending of a book is usually the death of an idea, and it's a callow writer indeed who isn't tempted to turn and take one last look at his characters or his thoughts before they pass beyond his control. It's a little like sending your youngest son out into the world with the admonition, "Write when you find work." The lump rises in your throat because you're a little afraid he's not ready.

Looking back quickly, we see a certain waspish obstinancy in these pieces, but if you feel that the basic theme is that every man is *not* entitled to his own opinion, you are wrong. If you feel as we do about cats, the Civil War, gourmets, and the horrid smartness of our times (the King James version of the Bible has recently been restructured in contemporary split-level style)—in other words, if you agree with us—then you are most assuredly entitled to your own opinion. Whatever else you may feel, you can't say we aren't fair.

ABOUT THE AUTHOR

Caskie Stinnett was born in Fauquier County, Virginia. After graduating from the College of William and Mary, he worked for newspapers in the South, served briefly in the Infantry during World War II with the rank of private, and then moved on to Washington, where he wrote War Production Board director Donald M. Nelson's monthly munitions production reports and, during the evenings, served as Washington correspondent for a theatrical weekly. It was in this yeasty atmosphere of explosives and entertainment that he began writing humor pieces for *The Saturday Evening Post,* an enterprise which he pursued most successfully for over ten years. He has also written humor and satire for *The Atlantic, Look, Esquire, Collier's, Holiday, Redbook,* and other magazines.

Mr. Stinnett's first book, *Will Not Run February 22nd,* was an act of vengeance against the railroads and summarized experiences accumulated while commuting from a Bucks County farm for nearly seven years. He later moved to Southern France, where in a villa above the Mediterranean he wrote his first novel, *Out of the Red,* a satire on the seasonal revolutions in Caribbean countries.

Now a resident of Princeton, New Jersey, he commutes to New York daily where he is executive editor of a large national magazine.